Iosias Jody (Ed.)

Alfredo Valente

Association football, Midfielder, Alpha Secondary
School, Vancouver Whitecaps (1986–2010)

Cred Press

Imprint

Permission is granted to copy, distribute and/or modify this document under the terms of the GNU Free Documentation License, Version 1.2 or any later version published by the Free Software Foundation; with no Invariant Sections, with the Front-Cover Texts, and with the Back- Cover Texts. A copy of the license is included in the section entitled "GNU Free Documentation License".

All parts of this book are extracted from Wikipedia, the free encyclopedia (www.wikipedia.org).

You can get detailed informations about the authors of this collection of articles at the end of this book. The editors (Ed.) of this book are no authors. They have not modified or extended the original texts.

Pictures published in this book can be under different licences than the GNU Free Documentation License. You can get detailed informations about the authors and licences of pictures at the end of this book.

The content of this book was generated collaboratively by volunteers. Please be advised that nothing found here has necessarily been reviewed by people with the expertise required to provide you with complete, accurate or reliable information. Some information in this book maybe misleading or wrong. The Publisher does not guarantee the validity of the information found here. If you need specific advice (f.e. in fields of medical, legal, financial, or risk management questions) please contact a professional who is licensed or knowledgeable in that area.

Any brand names and product names mentioned in this book are subject to trademark, brand or patent protection and are trademarks or registered trademarks of their respective holders. The use of brand names, product names, common names, trade names, product descriptions etc. even without a particular marking in this works is in no way to be construed to mean that such names may be regarded as unrestricted in respect of trademark and brand protection legislation and could thus be used by anyone.

Cover image: www.ingimage.com
Concerning the licence of the cover image please contact ingimage.

Publisher:
Cred Press is a trademark of
International Book Market Service Ltd., 17 Rue Meldrum, Beau Bassin, 1713-01 Mauritius
Email: info@bookmarketservice.com
Website: www.bookmarketservice.com

Published in 2011

Printed in: U.S.A., U.K., Germany. This book was not produced in Mauritius.

ISBN: 978-613-6-90523-5

Contents

Alfredo Valente	1
Association football	4
Midfielder	17
Alpha Secondary School	22
Vancouver Whitecaps (1986–2010)	24
Vancouver Metro Soccer League	33
Canada men's national under-20 soccer team	38
USL First Division	43
2005 United Soccer Leagues	49
2008 United Soccer Leagues	51
2009 United Soccer Leagues	55
Pan American Games	65

References

Article Sources and Contributors	70
Image Sources, Licenses and Contributors	73

Article Licenses

License	76

Alfredo Valente

Personal information	
Full name	Alfredo Valente
Date of birth	November 6, 1980
Place of birth	Burnaby, British Columbia, Canada
Height	5 ft 6 in (1.68 m)
Playing position	Midfielder
Club information	
Current club	Coquitlam Metro-Ford Wolves (Youth Head Coach)
Number	9
Youth career	
	Coquitlam Metro-Ford Soccer Club
–	Alpha Secondary School

Senior career*

Years	Team	Apps†	(Gls)†
1998-2008	Vancouver 86ers/Whitecaps	271	(35)

National team‡

1998	Canada U-20	1	(0)

Teams managed

2005-	Coquitlam Metro-Ford Wolves (Youth Head Coach)

* Senior club appearances and goals counted for the domestic league only and correct as of 27 September 2008.
† Appearances (Goals).
‡ National team caps and goals correct as of 19 May 2006

Alfredo Valente (born November 6, 1980 in Burnaby, British Columbia) is a former Canadian soccer midfielder who formerly played for the Vancouver Whitecaps of the USL First Division (USL-1). Valente played 11 seasons with the 86ers/Whitecaps organization, winning USL championships with the club in 2006 and 2008. He has also played indoor soccer with the Edmonton Drillers of the National Professional Soccer League (NPSL) early in his professional career.[1][2] Internationally, Valente has represented Canada with the under-18, under-20 and under-23 national teams.[1]

Early life

Growing up in Burnaby, British Columbia, a neighbouring city east of Vancouver, Valente began playing soccer at four years old. He joined the local youth and amateur Coquitlam Metro-Ford Soccer Club (CMFSC) program at 12 and debuted with the men's team in the Vancouver Metro Soccer League's Premier division three years later.[3]

Valente attended and graduated from Alpha Secondary School in Burnaby, where he also played for the high school's soccer club, the Aztecs leading them to a provincial championship.[1]

Playing career

Valente was drafted by the Vancouver 86ers (renamed to the Whitecaps in 2001) as the club's top pick in the 1998 A-League Player Draft.[1] He made his professional debut with the 86ers at 17-years-old in the USISL A-League and scored four goals in 14 games to be named Vancouver's top rookie that year in 1998.[1] He recorded his best season with the 86ers in 2000, leading the team in scoring with 10 goals.[1] In 2002, Valente led Vancouver in assists with 10, finishing tied for fifth overall in the USL First Division.[1]

Under the leadership of head coach Bob Lilley, hired in 2004, Valente's playing time began to decrease.[4] He did not get off the bench in the 2005 playoffs. The next season, however, after scoring a goal and an assist in the regular season, he started the title game against the Rochester Raging Rhinos; Valente helped the Whitecaps to their first USL championship, defeating Rochester 3–0.[4] Attempting to defend the Whitecaps league title in 2007, Valente appeared in 24 games, while starting in 14.[4] Coming off the bench in the club's two playoff games, Valente and the Whitecaps were defeated in the quarterfinals.

On February 7, 2008, the Whitecaps re-signed Valente for an 11th season.[4] At the time of the signing, he ranked seventh in Vancouver's all-time combined playoff and regular season scoring list with 32 goals and 35 assists in 234 games.[4] As Lilley was replaced by Icelandic Teitur Thordarson as head coach, Valente's playing time increased, becoming a regular starter.[5] After finishing with the second best regular season record in 2008, the Whitecaps won their second USL championship in three years, defeating the Puerto Rico Islanders 2–1 at Swangard Stadium on October 12, 2008. Valente was instrumental in the Whitecaps first goal in the 56th minute, directing a corner into the Islanders' box, where Charles Gbeke headed the ball in.[6]

Several months later, Valente was released by the Whitecaps, as the club chose against his 2009 contract option, on December 8, 2008, along with fellow veterans Steve Kindel, Jeff Clarke. Club president Bob Lenarduzzi and coach Thordarson cited "philosophical differences" for the roster changes.[7] Valente left the Whitecaps second all-time in franchise assists.[8] At the end of the 2008 season, Valente, Kindel and Clarke, all long-time members of the club, had voiced their concerns over Thordarson's coaching style in separate one-on-one meetings with him.[9]

Following his release from the Whitecaps, Valente rejoined the Coquitlam Metro-Ford Wolves of the Vancouver Metro Soccer League's Premier Division in 2009.[10] He has been involved with CMFSC, his old youth and amateur soccer club, since 2005 as youth coach and head coach of technical operations, as well.[3][11]

International play

Valente has represented Canada with the under-18, under-20 and Olympic under-23 national teams.[1] He played with Canada's U-18s for a tournament in Italy in March 1998[12] and the U-20s several months later in August 1998.[13] The following year, he was chosen to represent Canada at the 1999 Pan American Games in the United States.[12] In 2000, Valente went on tour with the Canadian Olympic team in Mexico as a 19-year-old.[14]

Personal life

Alfredo is married to Kristen Valente and has a son, Noah, born on December 19, 2007.[4]

Awards and accomplishments

- Named Vancouver 86ers Top Rookie in 1998.
- Led Vancouver Whitecaps in goals (10) in 2000.
- Led Vancouver Whitecaps in assists (10) in 2002.
- Won a USL First Division championship in 2006 and 2008.

Honors

Vancouver Whitecaps

- **USL First Division Championship (2):** 2006, 2008

References

[1] "#9 - Alfredo Valente" (http://www.uslsoccer.com/teams/2465825/22394-2465947/28597.html). USL First Division. . Retrieved 2009-09-09.

[2] "Wave rolls over Drllers in NPSL" (http://www.cbc.ca/sports/story/2000/11/11/drillers-wave001110.html). Canadian Broadcasting Corporation. 2000-11-11. . Retrieved 2009-09-10.

[3] "Coquitlam Metro-Ford Soccer motors into 25th year" (http://www.bclocalnews.com/tri_city_maple_ridge/tricitynews/sports/57036122.html). BC Local News. 2009-09-03. . Retrieved 2009-09-09.

[4] "Valente back for 11th season" (http://www.canada.com/theprovince/news/sports/story.html?id=6ee78bc8-2e14-4070-93ef-ceea2ec06c8e). The Province. 2008-02-08. . Retrieved 2009-09-09.

[5] "Steady Freddie at the ready" (http://www.canada.com/theprovince/news/sports/story.html?id=94d1f147-0710-4b85-b851-a6ec7c2b1e0d). The Province. 2008-09-11. . Retrieved 2009-09-10.

[6] "Gbeke leads Vancouver to second USL-1 title" (http://soccernet.espn.go.com/print?id=581341&type=story&cc=%). ESPN. 2008-10-12. . Retrieved 2009-09-09.

[7] Vancouver Whitecaps: 'Caps Part Ways with Three Veterans (http://www.whitecapsfc.com/archive/feature12080801.aspx) 8 December 2008

[8] "Veteran trio given cold shoulder" (http://www.canada.com/theprovince/news/sports/story.html?id=96c91882-2c46-424f-be3a-a90570822514). The Province. 2008-12-08. . Retrieved 2009-09-09.

[9] "Criticism of coach the cause" (http://www.canada.com/theprovince/news/sports/story.html?id=4909d025-adec-42d7-8acb-9dc8dbb452ef&p=1). The Province. 2008-12-11. . Retrieved 2009-09-10.

[10] "CMF Juventus, Sparta and Barca soccer Cup winners" (http://www.bclocalnews.com/tri_city_maple_ridge/tricitynews/sports/43799917.html). 2009-04-27. . Retrieved 2009-09-10.

[11] Coquitlam MFSC: Coaches (http://www.cmfsc.ca/Y-League/coaches.htm) Retrieved on 20 March 2009

[12] "Teen dreams of sunny Mexico" (http://slam.canoe.ca/SoccerNPSL/dec16_tee.html). Canadian Online Explorer. 1999-12-16. . Retrieved 2009-09-10.

[13] "United States U-20s men near qualifying for world championship." (http://www.soccertimes.com/usteams/1998/games/aug07a.htm). Soccertimes.com. 1998-08-07. . Retrieved 2009-09-10.

[14] "Drill's road rig shorthanded" (http://www.canoe.ca/SoccerNPSL/feb4_dri.html). Edmonton Sun. 2000-02-04. . Retrieved 2009-09-10.

External links

- USL profile of Alfredo Valente (http://www.uslsoccer.com/teams/2465825/22394-2465947/28597.html)

Association football

An attacking player (No. 10) attempts to kick the ball past the opposing team's goalkeeper and between the goalposts to score a goal.

Highest governing body	FIFA
Nickname(s)	Football, soccer, footy/footie, "the beautiful game", "the world game"
First played	Mid-19th century Britain
Characteristics	
Contact	Yes
Team members	11 per side
Mixed gender	Yes, separate competitions
Categorization	Team sport, ball sport
Equipment	Football or "soccer ball"
Venue	Football pitch
Olympic	1900

Association football, commonly known as **football** or **soccer**, is a sport played between two teams of eleven players with a spherical ball. At the turn of the 21st century the game was played by over 250 million players in over 200 countries, making it the world's most popular sport.[1][2][3][4]

The game is played on a rectangular field of grass or green artificial turf, with a goal in the middle of each of the short ends. The object of the game is to score by driving the ball into the opposing goal. In general play, the goalkeepers are the only players allowed to touch the ball with their hands or arms, while the field players typically use their feet to kick the ball into position, occasionally using their torso or head to intercept a ball in midair. The team that scores the most goals by the end of the match wins. If the score is tied at the end of the game, either a draw is declared or the game goes into extra time and/or a penalty shootout, depending on the format of the competition.

The Laws of the Game were originally codified in England by the Football Association in 1863 and have evolved since then. Association football is governed internationally by FIFA, which organises the FIFA World Cup every four years.[5]

Etymology

The rules of football were codified in England by the Football Association in 1863 and the name *association football* was coined to distinguish the game from the other forms of football played at the time, specifically rugby football. The term *soccer* originated in England, first appearing in the 1880s as an Oxford "-er" abbreviation of the word "association".[6]

Gameplay

A goalkeeper saving a close-range shot from inside the penalty area

Association football is played in accordance with a set of rules known as the Laws of the Game. The game is played using a spherical ball (of 71 cm (28 in) circumference in FIFA play), known as the *football* (or *soccer ball*). Two teams of eleven players each compete to get the ball into the other team's goal (between the posts and under the bar), thereby scoring a goal. The team that has scored more goals at the end of the game is the winner; if both teams have scored an equal number of goals then the game is a draw. Each team is led by a captain who has only one official responsibility as mandated the Laws of the Game: to be involved in the coin toss prior to kick-off or penalty kicks.[7]

The primary law is that players other than goalkeepers may not deliberately handle the ball with their hands or arms during play, though they do use their hands during a throw-in restart. Although players usually use their feet to move the ball around, they may use any part of their body (notably, "heading" with the forehead)[8] other than their hands or arms.[9] Within normal play, all players are free to play the ball in any direction and move throughout the pitch, though the ball cannot be received in an offside position.[10]

In typical game play, players attempt to create goal-scoring opportunities through individual control of the ball, such as by dribbling, passing the ball to a team-mate, and by taking shots at the goal, which is guarded by the opposing goalkeeper. Opposing players may try to regain control of the ball by intercepting a pass or through tackling the opponent in possession of the ball; however, physical contact between opponents is restricted. Football is generally a free-flowing game, with play stopping only when the ball has left the field of play or when play is stopped by the referee for an infringement of the rules. After a stoppage, play recommences with a specified restart.[11]

At a professional level, most matches produce only a few goals. For example, the 2005–06 season of the English Premier League produced an average of 2.48 goals per match.[12] The Laws of the Game do not specify any player positions other than goalkeeper,[13] but a number of specialised roles have evolved. Broadly, these include three main categories: strikers, or forwards, whose main task is to score goals; defenders, who specialise in preventing their opponents from scoring; and midfielders, who dispossess the opposition and keep possession of the ball in order to pass it to the forwards on their team. Players in these positions are referred to as outfield players, in order to

A goalkeeper dives to stop the ball from entering his goal

distinguish them from the goalkeeper. These positions are further subdivided according to the area of the field in which the player spends most time. For example, there are central defenders, and left and right midfielders. The ten outfield players may be arranged in any combination. The number of players in each position determines the style of the team's play; more forwards and fewer defenders creates a more aggressive and offensive-minded game, while the reverse creates a slower, more defensive style of play. While players typically spend most of the game in a specific position, there are few restrictions on player movement, and players can switch positions at any time.[14] The layout of a team's players is known as a *formation*. Defining the team's formation and tactics is usually the prerogative of the team's manager.[15]

History

Games revolving around the kicking of a ball have been played in many countries throughout history. According to FIFA, the "The very earliest form of the game for which there is scientific evidence was an exercise from a military manual dating back to the second and third centuries BC in China."[16] The modern rules of association football are based on the mid-19th century efforts to standardise the widely varying forms of football played at the public schools of England. The history of football in England dates back to at least the eighth century.[17]

England playing Scotland in the first-ever international football game (The Oval, 1872)

The Cambridge Rules, first drawn up at Cambridge University in 1848, were particularly influential in the development of subsequent codes, including association football. The Cambridge Rules were written at Trinity College, Cambridge, at a meeting attended by representatives from Eton, Harrow, Rugby, Winchester and Shrewsbury schools. They were not universally adopted. During the 1850s, many clubs unconnected to schools or universities were formed throughout the English-speaking world, to play various forms of football. Some came up with their own distinct codes of rules, most notably the Sheffield Football Club, formed by former public school pupils in 1857,[18] which led to formation of a Sheffield FA in 1867. In 1862, John Charles Thring of Uppingham School also devised an influential set of rules.[19]

The Royal Engineers team who reached the first FA Cup final in 1872

These ongoing efforts contributed to the formation of The Football Association (The FA) in 1863, which first met on the morning of 26 October 1863 at the Freemasons' Tavern in Great Queen Street, London.[20] The only school to be represented on this occasion was Charterhouse. The Freemason's Tavern was the setting for five more meetings between October and December, which eventually produced the first comprehensive set of rules. At the final meeting, the first FA treasurer, the representative from Blackheath, withdrew his club from the FA over the removal of two draft rules at the previous meeting: the first allowed for running with the ball in hand; the second for obstructing such a run by hacking (kicking an opponent in the shins), tripping and holding. Other English rugby football clubs followed this lead and did not join the FA, or subsequently left the FA and instead in 1871 formed the Rugby Football Union. The eleven remaining clubs, under the charge of Ebenezer Cobb Morley, went on to ratify the original thirteen laws of the game.[20] These rules included handling of the ball by "marks" and the lack of a crossbar, rules which made it remarkably similar to Victorian rules football being developed at that time in Australia. The Sheffield FA played by its own rules until the 1870s with the FA absorbing some of its rules until there was little difference between the games.[21]

The laws of the game are currently determined by the International Football Association Board (IFAB).[22] The Board was formed in 1886[23] after a meeting in Manchester of The Football Association, the Scottish Football Association, the Football Association of Wales, and the Irish Football Association. The world's oldest football competition is the FA Cup, which was founded by C. W. Alcock and has been contested by English teams since

1872. The first official international football match took place in 1872 between Scotland and England in Glasgow, again at the instigation of C. W. Alcock. England is home to the world's first football league, which was founded in Birmingham in 1888 by Aston Villa director William McGregor.[24] The original format contained 12 clubs from the Midlands and the North of England. FIFA, the international football body, was formed in Paris in 1904 and declared that they would adhere to Laws of the Game of the Football Association.[25] The growing popularity of the international game led to the admittance of FIFA representatives to the International Football Association Board in 1913. The board currently consists of four representatives from FIFA and one representative from each of the four British associations.[26]

Today, football is played at a professional level all over the world. Millions of people regularly go to football stadiums to follow their favourite teams,[27] while billions more watch the game on television or on the internet.[28] A very large number of people also play football at an amateur level. According to a survey conducted by FIFA published in 2001, over 240 million people from more than 200 countries regularly play football.[29] Football has the highest global television audience in sport.[30]

In many parts of the world football evokes great passions and plays an important role in the life of individual fans, local communities, and even nations. The Côte d'Ivoire national football team helped secure a truce to the nation's civil war in 2006[31] and it helped further reduce tensions between government and rebel forces in 2007 by playing a match in the rebel capital of Bouaké, an occasion that brought both armies together peacefully for the first time.[32] By contrast, football is widely considered to be the final proximate cause in the Football War in June 1969 between El Salvador and Honduras.[33] The sport also exacerbated tensions at the beginning of the Yugoslav wars of the 1990s, when a match between Dinamo Zagreb and Red Star Belgrade degenerated into rioting in March 1990.[34]

Laws

There are 17 laws in the official Laws of the Game. The same laws are designed to apply to all levels of football, although certain modifications for groups such as juniors, seniors, women and people with physical disabilities are permitted. The laws are often framed in broad terms, which allow flexibility in their application depending on the nature of the game. The Laws of the Game are published by FIFA, but are maintained by the International Football Association Board (IFAB), not FIFA itself.[35] In addition to the seventeen laws, numerous IFAB decisions and other directives contribute to the regulation of football. The most complex of the laws is offside. The offside law limits the ability of attacking players to receive the ball when closer to the opponent's goal line than: the ball itself; the second-to-last defending player (which can include the goalkeeper); and the half-way line.[10]

Players, equipment, and officials

Each team consists of a maximum of eleven players (excluding substitutes), one of whom must be the goalkeeper. Competition rules may state a minimum number of players required to constitute a team, which is usually seven. Goalkeepers are the only players allowed to play the ball with their hands or arms, provided they do so within the penalty area in front of their own goal. Though there are a variety of positions in which the outfield (non-goalkeeper) players are strategically placed by a coach, these positions are not defined or required by the Laws.[13]

The basic equipment or *kit* players are required to wear includes a shirt, shorts, socks, footwear and adequate shin guards. Headgear is not a required piece of basic equipment, but players today may choose to wear it to protect themselves from head injury. Players are forbidden to wear or use anything that is dangerous to themselves or another player, such as jewellery or watches. The goalkeeper must wear clothing that is easily distinguishable from that worn by the other players and the match officials.[36]

A number of players may be replaced by substitutes during the course of the game. The maximum number of substitutions permitted in most competitive international and domestic league games is three, though the permitted number may vary in other competitions or in friendly matches. Common reasons for a substitution include injury, tiredness, ineffectiveness, a tactical switch, or timewasting at the end of a finely poised game. In standard adult matches, a player who has been substituted may not take further part in a match.[37] IFAB recommends that "that a match should not continue if there are fewer than seven players in either team." Any decision regarding points awarded for abandoned games is left to the individual football associations.[38]

A game is officiated by a referee, who has "full authority to enforce the Laws of the Game in connection with the match to which he has been appointed" (Law 5), and whose decisions are final. The referee is assisted by two assistant referees. In many high-level games there is also a fourth official who assists the referee and may replace another official should the need arise.[39]

Pitch

As the Laws were formulated in England, and were initially administered solely by the four British football associations within IFAB, the standard dimensions of a football pitch were originally expressed in imperial units. The Laws now express dimensions with approximate metric equivalents (followed by traditional units in brackets), though popular use tends to continue to use traditional units in English-speaking countries with a relatively recent history of metrication, such as Britain.[40]

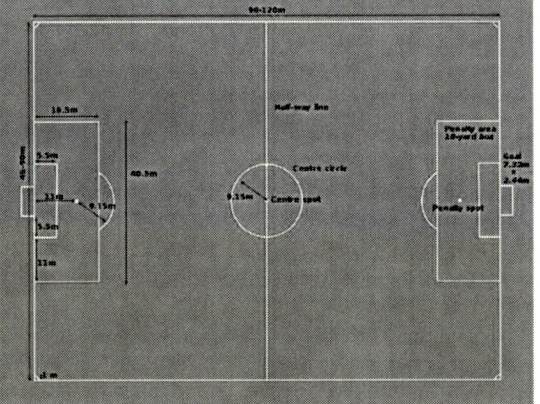

Standard pitch measurements (See Imperial version)

The length of the pitch for international adult matches is in the range of 100–110 m (110–120 yd) and the width is in the range of 64–75 m (70–80 yd). Fields for non-international matches may be 91–120 m (100–130 yd) length and 45–91 m (50–101 yd) in width, provided that the pitch does not become square. Although in 2008, the IFAB initially approved a fixed size of 105 m long and 68 m wide as a standard pitch dimension for A international matches,[41] this decision was later put on hold and was never actually implemented.[42]

The longer boundary lines are *touchlines*, while the shorter boundaries (on which the goals are placed) are *goal lines*. A rectangular goal is positioned at the middle of each goal line.[43] The inner edges of the vertical goal posts must be 7.32 m (8 yd) apart, and the lower edge of the horizontal crossbar supported by the goal posts must be 2.44 m (8 ft) above the ground. Nets are usually placed behind the goal, but are not required by the Laws.[44]

In front of each goal is an area known as the penalty area. This area is marked by the goal line, two lines starting on the goal line 16.5 m (18 yd) from the goalposts and extending 16.5 m (18 yd) into the pitch perpendicular to the goal line, and a line joining them. This area has a number of functions, the most prominent being to mark where the goalkeeper may handle the ball and where a penalty foul by a member of the defending team becomes punishable by a penalty kick. Other markings define the position of the ball or players at kick-offs, goal kicks, penalty kicks and corner kicks.[45]

Duration and tie-breaking methods

A standard adult football match consists of two periods of 45 minutes each, known as halves. Each half runs continuously, meaning that the clock is not stopped when the ball is out of play. There is usually a 15-minute half-time break between halves. The end of the match is known as full-time.[46] The referee is the official timekeeper for the match, and may make an allowance for time lost through substitutions, injured players requiring attention, or other stoppages. This added time is commonly referred to as *stoppage time* or *injury time*, and is at the sole discretion of the referee. The referee alone signals the end of the match. In matches where a fourth official is appointed, toward the end of the half the referee signals how many minutes of stoppage time he intends to add. The fourth official then informs the players and spectators by holding up a board showing this number. The signalled stoppage time may be further extended by the referee.[46] Added time was introduced because of an incident which happened in 1891 during a match between Stoke and Aston Villa. Trailing 1–0 and with just two minutes remaining, Stoke were awarded a penalty. Villa's goalkeeper kicked the ball out of the ground, and by the time the ball had been recovered, the 90 minutes had elapsed and the game was over.[47] The same law also stands that the duration of either half is extended until the penalty kick to be taken or retaken is completed, thus no game shall end with a penalty to be taken.[48]

In league competitions, games may end in a draw, but in some knockout competitions if a game is tied at the end of regulation time it may go into extra time, which consists of two further 15-minute periods. If the score is still tied after extra time, some competitions allow the use of penalty shootouts (known officially in the Laws of the Game as "kicks from the penalty mark") to determine which team will progress to the next stage of the tournament. Goals scored during extra time periods count toward the final score of the game, but kicks from the penalty mark are only used to decide the team that progresses to the next part of the tournament (with goals scored in a penalty shootout not making up part of the final score).[7]

In competitions using two-legged matches, each team competes at home once, with an aggregate score from the two matches deciding which team progresses. Where aggregates are equal, the away goals rule may be used to determine the winners, in which case the winner is the team that scored the most goals in the leg played away from home. If the result is still equal, kicks from the penalty mark are required.[7]

In the late 1990s and early 2000s, the IFAB experimented with ways of creating a winner without requiring a penalty shootout, which was often seen as an undesirable way to end a match. These involved rules ending a game in extra time early, either when the first goal in extra time was scored (*golden goal*), or if one team held a lead at the end of the first period of extra time (*silver goal*). Golden goal was used at the World Cup in 1998 and 2002. The first World Cup game decided by a golden goal was France's victory over Paraguay in 1998. Germany was the first nation to score a golden goal in a major competition, beating Czech Republic in the final of Euro 1996. Silver goal was used in Euro 2004. Both these experiments have been discontinued by IFAB.[49]

Ball in and out of play

Under the Laws, the two basic states of play during a game are *ball in play* and *ball out of play*. From the beginning of each playing period with a kick-off until the end of the playing period, the ball is in play at all times, except when either the ball leaves the field of play, or play is stopped by the referee. When the ball becomes out of play, play is restarted by one of eight restart methods depending on how it went out of play:

- Kick-off: following a goal by the opposing team, or to begin each period of play.[11]
- Throw-in: when the ball has crossed the touchline; awarded to opposing team to that which last touched the ball.[50]
- Goal kick: when the ball has wholly crossed the goal line without a goal having been scored and having last been touched by a player of the attacking team; awarded to defending team.[51]
- Corner kick: when the ball has wholly crossed the goal line without a goal having been scored and having last been touched by a player of the defending team; awarded to attacking team.[52]

A player takes a free kick, while the opposition form a "wall" to try to deflect the ball

- Indirect free kick: awarded to the opposing team following "non-penal" fouls, certain technical infringements, or when play is stopped to caution or send-off an opponent without a specific foul having occurred. A goal may not be scored directly (without the ball first touching another player) from an indirect free kick.[53]
- Direct free kick: awarded to fouled team following certain listed "penal" fouls.[53] A goal may be scored directly from a direct free kick.
- Penalty kick: awarded to the fouled team following a foul usually punishable by a direct free kick but that has occurred within their opponent's penalty area.[54]
- Dropped-ball: occurs when the referee has stopped play for any other reason, such as a serious injury to a player, interference by an external party, or a ball becoming defective. This restart is uncommon in adult games.[11]

Misconduct

Players are cautioned with a yellow card, and sent off with a red card. These colours were first introduced at the 1970 FIFA World Cup and used consistently since.

A player scores a penalty kick given after an offence is committed inside the penalty area

A foul occurs when a player commits an offence listed in the Laws of the Game while the ball is in play. The offences that constitute a foul are listed in Law 12. Handling the ball deliberately, tripping an opponent, or pushing an opponent, are examples of "penal fouls", punishable by a direct free kick or penalty kick depending on where the offence occurred. Other fouls are punishable by an indirect free kick.[9] The referee may punish a player or substitute's misconduct by a caution (yellow card) or sending-off (red card). A second yellow card at the same game leads to a red card, and therefore to a sending-off. A player given a yellow card is said to have been "booked", the referee writing the player's name in his official notebook. If a player has been sent off, no substitute can be brought on in their place. Misconduct may occur at any time, and while the offences that constitute misconduct are listed, the definitions are broad. In particular, the offence of "unsporting behaviour" may be used to deal with most events that violate the spirit of the game, even if they are not listed as specific offences. A referee can show a yellow or red card to a player, substitute or substituted player. Non-players such as managers and support staff cannot be shown the yellow or red card, but may be expelled from the technical area if they fail to conduct themselves in a responsible manner.[9]

Rather than stopping play, the referee may allow play to continue if doing so will benefit the team against which an offence has been committed. This is known as "playing an advantage".[55] The referee may "call back" play and penalise the original offence if the anticipated advantage does not ensue within "a few seconds". Even if an offence is not penalised due to advantage being played, the offender may still be sanctioned for misconduct at the next stoppage of play.[56]

Governing bodies

The recognised international governing body of football (and associated games, such as futsal and beach soccer) is the Fédération Internationale de Football Association (FIFA). The FIFA headquarters are located in Zurich. Six regional confederations are associated with FIFA; these are:[57]

- Asia: Asian Football Confederation (AFC)
- Africa: Confederation of African Football (CAF)
- Europe: Union of European Football Associations (UEFA)
- North/Central America & Caribbean: Confederation of North, Central American and Caribbean Association Football (CONCACAF)
- Oceania: Oceania Football Confederation (OFC)
- South America: Confederación Sudamericana de Fútbol/Confederação Sul-americana de Futebol (South American Football Confederation; CONMEBOL)

National associations oversee football within individual countries. These are generally synonymous with sovereign states, (for example: the Fédération Camerounaise de Football in Cameroon) but also include a smaller number of associations responsible for sub-national entities or autonomous regions (for example the Scottish Football Association in Scotland). 208 national associations are affiliated both with FIFA and with their respective continental confederations.[57]

While FIFA is responsible for arranging competitions and most rules related to international competition, the actual Laws of the Game are set by the International Football Association Board, where each of the UK Associations has one vote, while FIFA collectively has four votes.[26]

International competitions

The major international competition in football is the World Cup, organised by FIFA. This competition takes place over a four-year period. More than 190 national teams compete in qualifying tournaments within the scope of continental confederations for a place in the finals. The finals tournament, which is held every four years, involves 32 national teams competing over a four-week period.[58] The most recent tournament, the 2010 FIFA World Cup, was held in South Africa from 11 June to 11 July.[59]

A minute's silence before an international match

There has been a football tournament at every Summer Olympic Games since 1900, except at the 1932 games in Los Angeles.[60] Before the inception of the World Cup, the Olympics (especially during the 1920s) had the same status as the World Cup. Originally, the event was for amateurs only,[25] however, since the 1984 Summer Olympics professional players have been permitted, albeit with certain restrictions which prevent countries from fielding their strongest sides. Currently, the Olympic men's tournament is played at Under-23 level. In the past the Olympics have allowed a restricted number of over-age players per team;[61] but that practice ceased in the 2008 Olympics. A women's tournament was added in 1996; in contrast to the men's event, full international sides without age restrictions play the women's Olympic tournament.[62]

After the World Cup, the most important international football competitions are the continental championships, which are organised by each continental confederation and contested between national teams. These are the European Championship (UEFA), the Copa América (CONMEBOL), African Cup of Nations (CAF), the Asian Cup (AFC), the CONCACAF Gold Cup (CONCACAF) and the OFC Nations Cup (OFC). The FIFA Confederations Cup is contested by the winners of all 6 continental championships, the current FIFA World Cup champions and the country which is hosting the Confederations Cup. This is generally regarded as a warm up tournament for the upcoming FIFA World Cup and does not carry the same prestige as the World Cup itself. The most prestigious competitions in club football are the respective continental championships, which are generally contested between national champions, for example the UEFA Champions League in Europe and the Copa Libertadores de América in South America. The winners of each continental competition contest the FIFA Club World Cup.[63]

Domestic competitions

The governing bodies in each country operate league systems in a domestic season, normally comprising several divisions, in which the teams gain points throughout the season depending on results. Teams are placed into tables, placing them in order according to points accrued. Most commonly, each team plays every other team in its league at home and away in each season, in a round-robin tournament. At the end of a season, the top team is declared the champion. The top few teams may be promoted to a higher division, and one or more of the teams finishing at the bottom are relegated to a lower division.[64] The teams finishing at the top of a country's league may be eligible also to play in international club competitions in the following season. The main exceptions to this system occur in some Latin American leagues, which divide football championships into two sections named Apertura and Clausura (Spanish for *Opening* and *Closing*), awarding a champion for each.[65] The majority of countries supplement the league system with one or more "cup" competitions organised on a knock-out basis.

Two players trying to win the ball

Some countries' top divisions feature highly paid star players; in smaller countries and lower divisions, players may be part-timers with a second job, or amateurs. The five top European leagues – the Premier League (England),[66] La Liga (Spain), Serie A (Italy), the Bundesliga (Germany) and Ligue 1 (France) – attract most of the world's best players and each of the leagues has a total wage cost in excess of £600 million/€763 million/$1.185 billion.[67]

Women's association football

Women have been playing association football since the first recorded women's game in 1895 in North London. It has traditionally been associated with charity games and physical exercise, particularly in the United Kingdom.[68] This perception began to change in the 1970s with the breakthrough of organised women's association football. Association football is the most prominent team sport for women in several countries, and one of the few women's team sports with professional leagues.

The growth in women's football has seen major competitions being launched at both national and international level mirroring the male competitions. Women's football faced many struggles throughout its fight for right. It had a "golden age" in the United Kingdom in the early 1920s when crowds reached 50,000 at some matches;[69] this was stopped on 5 December 1921 when England's Football Association voted to ban the game from grounds used by its member clubs. The FA's ban was rescinded in December 1969 with UEFA voting to officially recognise women's football in 1971.[68] The FIFA Women's World Cup was inaugurated in 1991 and has been held every four years since.[70]

See also

- Association football culture
- Association football tactics and skills
- List of association football clubs
- List of women's association football clubs
- List of men's national association football teams
- List of top association football goal scorers
- List of top association football goal scorers by country
- Lists of association football players
- Paralympic association football
- Variants of association football

References

[1] "Overview of Soccer" (http://www.britannica.com/EBchecked/topic/550852/football). Encyclopædia Britannica. . Retrieved 2008-06-04.

[2] Guttman, Allen (1993). "The Diffusion of Sports and the Problem of Cultural Imperialism" (http://books.google.com/books?id=tQY5wxQDn5gC&pg=PA129&lpg=PA129&dq=world's+most+popular+team+sport&source=web&ots=6ns3wVUEGV&sig=SZPKYSDMJBrO1uV4mPxNbKyAuJY#PPA129,M1). In Eric Dunning, Joseph A. Maguire, Robert E. Pearton. *The Sports Process: A Comparative and Developmental Approach*. Champaign: Human Kinetics. p. 129. ISBN 0-88011-624-2. . Retrieved 2008-01-26. "the game is complex enough not to be invented independently by many preliterate cultures and yet simple enough to become the world's most popular team sport"

[3] Dunning, Eric (1999). "The development of soccer as a world game" (http://books.google.com/books?id=X3lX_LVBaToC&pg=PA105&lpg=PA105&dq=world's+most+popular+team+sport&source=web&ots=ehee9Lr9o1&sig=nyvDhcrPoR8lXhYKE7k4CZYg_qU#PPA103,M1). *Sport Matters: Sociological Studies of Sport, Violence and Civilisation*. London: Routledge. p. 103. ISBN 0-415-06413-9. . Retrieved 2008-01-26. "During the twentieth century, soccer emerged as the world's most popular team sport"

[4] Mueller, Frederick; Cantu; Van Camp, Steven (1996). "Team Sports" (http://books.google.com/books?id=XG6AIHLtyaUC&pg=PA57&lpg=PA57&dq=soccer+most+popular+team+sport&source=web&ots=QzydYB5Am0&sig=w_ouIgmegjytYFfWy7k92guTNfU#PPA57,M1). *Catastrophic Injuries in High School and College Sports*. Champaign: Human Kinetics. p. 57. ISBN 0-87322-674-7. . Retrieved 2008-01-26. "Soccer is the most popular sport in the world and is an industry worth over US$400 billion world wide. 80% of this is generated in Europe, though its popularity is growing in the United States. It has been estimated that there were 22 million soccer players in the world in the early 1980s, and that number is increasing. In the United States soccer is now a major sport at both the high school and college levels"

[5] "2002 FIFA World Cup TV Coverage" (http://web.archive.org/web/20061230124633/http://www.fifa.com/en/marketing/newmedia/index/0,3509,10,00.html). FIFA. 2006-12-05. Archived from the original (http://www.fifa.com/en/marketing/newmedia/index/0,3509,10,00.html) on 2006-12-30. . Retrieved 2008-01-06.

[6] Mazumdar, Partha (2006-06-05). "The Yanks are Coming: A U.S. World Cup Preview" (http://www.usembassy.org.uk/rss/transcripts/worldcup2006a.html). Embassy of the United States in London. . Retrieved 2009-06-06.
[7] IFAB. "Procedures to determine the winner of a match or home-and-away" (http://www.fifa.com/mm/document/affederation/generic/81/42/36/lawsofthegame_2010_11_e.pdf) (PDF). *Laws of the Game 2010/2011*. FIFA. p. 51–52. . Retrieved 2011-03-04.
[8] "How to head a football)" (http://expertfootball.com/training/heading.php). . Retrieved 2011-01-03.
[9] "Laws of the game (Law 12)" (http://web.archive.org/web/20071011115718/http://fifa.com/flash/lotg/football/en/Laws12_02.htm). FIFA. Archived from the original (http://www.fifa.com/flash/lotg/football/en/Laws12_02.htm) on 11 October 2007. . Retrieved 2007-09-24.
[10] IFAB. "Law 11 – Offside" (http://www.fifa.com/mm/document/affederation/generic/81/42/36/lawsofthegame_2010_11_e.pdf) (PDF). *Laws of the Game 2010/2011*. FIFA. p. 31. . Retrieved 2011-03-04.
[11] "Laws of the game (Law 8)" (http://web.archive.org/web/20070913142456/http://fifa.com/flash/lotg/football/en/Laws8_01.htm). FIFA. Archived from the original (http://www.fifa.com/flash/lotg/football/en/Laws8_01.htm) on 2007-09-13. . Retrieved 2007-09-24.
[12] "England Premiership (2005/2006)" (http://www.sportpress.com/stats/en/738_england_premiership_2005_2006/11_league_summary.html). *Sportpress.com*. . Retrieved 2007-06-05.
[13] "Laws of the game (Law 3–Number of Players)" (http://web.archive.org/web/20070913142527/http://fifa.com/flash/lotg/football/en/Laws3_01.htm). FIFA. Archived from the original (http://www.fifa.com/flash/lotg/football/en/Laws3_01.htm) on 2007-09-13. . Retrieved 2007-09-24.
[14] "Positions guide, Who is in a team?" (http://news.bbc.co.uk/sport1/hi/football/rules_and_equipment/4196830.stm). *BBC Sport* (BBC). 2005-09-01. . Retrieved 2007-09-24.
[15] "Formations" (http://news.bbc.co.uk/sport1/hi/football/rules_and_equipment/4197420.stm). *BBC Sport* (BBC). 2005-09-01. . Retrieved 2007-09-24.
[16] "History of Football" (http://www.fifa.com/classicfootball/history/game/historygame1.html). FIFA. . Retrieved 2006-11-20.
[17] "History of Football – Britain, the home of Football" (http://www.fifa.com/classicfootball/history/game/historygame2.html). FIFA. . Retrieved 2006-11-20.
[18] Harvey, Adrian (2005). *Football, the first hundred years*. London: Routledge. p. 126. ISBN 0-415-35018-2.
[19] Winner, David (2005-03-28). "The hands-off approach to a man's game" (http://www.timesonline.co.uk/article/0,,27-1544006,00.html). *The Times* (London). . Retrieved 2007-10-07.
[20] "History of the FA" (http://web.archive.org/web/20050407161619/http://www.thefa.com/TheFA/TheOrganisation/Postings/2004/03/HISTORY_OF_THE_FA.htm). Football Association (FA). Archived from the original (http://www.thefa.com/TheFA/TheOrganisation/Postings/2004/03/HISTORY_OF_THE_FA.htm) on 7 April 2005. . Retrieved 2007-10-09.
[21] Young, Percy M. (1964). *Football in Sheffield*. S. Paul. pp. 28–29.
[22] "IFAB: 125 years and still going strong" (http://www.fifa.com/aboutfifa/federation/ifab/news/newsid=1379963.html). FIFA. 2011-02-10. . Retrieved 2011-03-04.
[23] "The International FA Board" (http://web.archive.org/web/20070422035010/http://access.fifa.com/en/history/history/0,3504,3,00.html). FIFA. Archived from the original (http://access.fifa.com/en/history/history/0,3504,3,00.html) on 2007-04-22. . Retrieved 2007-09-02.
[24] "The History Of The Football League" (http://www.football-league.co.uk/page/History/HistoryDetail/0,,10794~1357277,00.html). Football League. 2010-09-22. . Retrieved 2011-03-04.
[25] "Where it all began" (http://web.archive.org/web/20070608215029/http://access.fifa.com/en/history/history/0,3504,4,00.html). FIFA. Archived from the original (http://access.fifa.com/en/history/history/0,3504,4,00.html) on 2007-06-08. . Retrieved 2007-06-08.
[26] "The IFAB: How it works" (http://www.fifa.com/aboutfifa/federation/ifab/howitworks.html). FIFA. . Retrieved 2011-03-04.
[27] Ingle, Sean; Glendenning, Barry (2003-10-09). "Baseball or Football: which sport gets the higher attendance?" (http://football.guardian.co.uk/news/theknowledge/0,9204,1059366,00.html). *The Guardian* (UK). . Retrieved 2006-06-05.
[28] "TV Data" (http://web.archive.org/web/20070922225713/http://fifa.com/aboutfifa/marketingtv/factsfigures/tvdata.html). FIFA. Archived from the original (http://www.fifa.com/aboutfifa/marketingtv/factsfigures/tvdata.html) on 22 September 2007. . Retrieved 2007-09-02.
[29] "FIFA Survey: approximately 250 million footballers worldwide" (http://web.archive.org/web/20060915133001/http://access.fifa.com/infoplus/IP-199_01E_big-count.pdf) (PDF). FIFA. Archived from the original (http://access.fifa.com/infoplus/IP-199_01E_big-count.pdf) on 2006-09-15. . Retrieved 2006-09-15.
[30] "2006 FIFA World Cup broadcast wider, longer and farther than ever before" (http://www.fifa.com/aboutfifa/marketing/factsfigures/tvdata.html). FIFA. . Retrieved 2009-10-11.
[31] Stormer, Neil (2006-06-20). "More than a game" (http://www.commongroundnews.org/article.php?sid=1&id=2079). *Common Ground News Service*. . Retrieved 2010-03-02.
[32] Austin, Merrill (2007-07-10). "Best Feet Forward" (http://www.vanityfair.com/culture/features/2007/07/ivorycoast200707). *Vanity Fair*. . Retrieved 2010-03-02.
[33] Dart, James; Bandini, Paolo (2007-02-21). "Has football ever started a war?" (http://football.guardian.co.uk/theknowledge/story/0,,2017161,00.html). *The Guardian* (London). . Retrieved 2007-09-24.
[34] Drezner, Daniel (2006-06-04). "The Soccer Wars" (http://www.washingtonpost.com/wp-dyn/content/article/2006/06/02/AR2006060201401.html). *The Washington Post*: p. B01. . Retrieved 2008-05-21.

[35] "Laws Of The Game" (http://www.fifa.com/worldfootball/lawsofthegame.html). FIFA. . Retrieved 2007-09-02.
[36] "Laws of the game (Law 4–Players' Equipment)" (http://web.archive.org/web/20070913141601/http://fifa.com/flash/lotg/football/en/Laws4_01.htm). FIFA. Archived from the original (http://www.fifa.com/flash/lotg/football/en/Laws4_01.htm) on 2007-09-13. . Retrieved 2007-09-24.
[37] "Laws of the game (Law 3–Substitution procedure)" (http://web.archive.org/web/20071011144947/http://fifa.com/flash/lotg/football/en/Laws3_02.htm). FIFA. Archived from the original (http://www.fifa.com/flash/lotg/football/en/Laws3_02.htm) on 11 October 2007. . Retrieved 2007-09-24.
[38] IFAB. "Law 3 – The Number of Players" (http://www.fifa.com/mm/document/affederation/generic/81/42/36/lawsofthegame_2010_11_e.pdf) (PDF). *Laws of the Game 2010/2011*. FIFA. p. 62. . Retrieved 2011-03-04.
[39] "Laws of the game (Law 5–The referee)" (http://web.archive.org/web/20070913141909/http://fifa.com/flash/lotg/football/en/Laws5_01.htm). FIFA. Archived from the original (http://www.fifa.com/flash/lotg/football/en/Laws5_01.htm) on 2007-09-13. . Retrieved 2007-09-24.
[40] Summers, Chris (2004-09-02). "Will we ever go completely metric?" (http://news.bbc.co.uk/1/hi/magazine/3934353.stm). *BBC news* (BBC). . Retrieved 2007-10-07.
[41] "FIFA MEDIA Release (2008-03-08) Goal-line technology put on ice" (http://www.fifa.com/aboutfifa/federation/bodies/media/newsid=707751.html). FIFA. 2008-03-08. . Retrieved 2010-06-19.
[42] "FIFA Amendments to the Laws of the Game, 2008" (http://www.fifa.com/mm/document/affederation/administration/77/82/55/circularno.1145-amendmentstothelawsofthegame-2008.pdf) (PDF). FIFA. . Retrieved 2011-03-04.
[43] "Laws of the game (Law 1.1–The field of play)" (http://web.archive.org/web/20070913142202/http://fifa.com/flash/lotg/football/en/Laws1_01.htm). FIFA. Archived from the original (http://www.fifa.com/flash/lotg/football/en/Laws1_01.htm) on 13 September 2007. . Retrieved 2007-09-24.
[44] "Laws of the game (Law 1.4–The Field of play)" (http://web.archive.org/web/20071011144942/http://fifa.com/flash/lotg/football/en/Laws1_04.htm). FIFA. Archived from the original (http://www.fifa.com/flash/lotg/football/en/Laws1_04.htm) on 11 October 2007. . Retrieved 2007-09-24.
[45] "Laws of the game (Law 1.3–The field of play)" (http://web.archive.org/web/20071011084145/http://fifa.com/flash/lotg/football/en/Laws1_03.htm). FIFA. Archived from the original (http://www.fifa.com/flash/lotg/football/en/Laws1_03.htm) on 11 October 2007. . Retrieved 2007-09-24.
[46] "Laws of the game (Law 7.2–The duration of the match)" (http://web.archive.org/web/20071011144952/http://fifa.com/flash/lotg/football/en/Laws7_02.htm). FIFA. Archived from the original (http://www.fifa.com/flash/lotg/football/en/Laws7_02.htm) on 2007-10-11. . Retrieved 2007-09-24.
[47] The Sunday Times *Illustrated History Of Football* Reed International Books Limited 1996. p.11 ISBN 1-85613-341-9
[48] "Laws of the game (Law 7.3–The duration of the match)" (http://web.archive.org/web/20080603064822/http://www.fifa.com/flash/lotg/football/en/Laws7_03.htm). FIFA. Archived from the original (http://www.fifa.com/flash/lotg/football/en/Laws7_03.htm) on 3 June 2008. . Retrieved 2010-03-03.
[49] Collett, Mike (2004-07-02). "Time running out for silver goal" (http://www.rediff.com/sports/2004/jul/02silver.htm). Rediff.com. . Retrieved 2007-10-07.
[50] "Laws of the game (Law 15–The Throw-in)" (http://web.archive.org/web/20070913142556/http://fifa.com/flash/lotg/football/en/Laws15_01.htm). FIFA. Archived from the original (http://www.fifa.com/flash/lotg/football/en/Laws15_01.htm) on 2007-09-13. . Retrieved 2007-10-14.
[51] "Laws of the game (Law 16–The Goal Kick)" (http://web.archive.org/web/20070913141725/http://fifa.com/flash/lotg/football/en/Laws16_01.htm). FIFA. Archived from the original (http://www.fifa.com/flash/lotg/football/en/Laws16_01.htm) on 2007-09-13. . Retrieved 2007-10-14.
[52] "Laws of the game (Law 17–The Corner Kick)" (http://web.archive.org/web/20070913142324/http://fifa.com/flash/lotg/football/en/Laws17_01.htm). FIFA. Archived from the original (http://www.fifa.com/flash/lotg/football/en/Laws17_01.htm) on 2007-09-13. . Retrieved 2007-10-14.
[53] "Laws of the game (Law 13–Free Kicks)" (http://web.archive.org/web/20070913142645/http://fifa.com/flash/lotg/football/en/Laws13_01.htm). FIFA. Archived from the original (http://www.fifa.com/flash/lotg/football/en/Laws13_01.htm) on 2007-09-13. . Retrieved 2007-10-14.
[54] "Laws of the game (Law 14–The Penalty Kick)" (http://web.archive.org/web/20070913142717/http://fifa.com/flash/lotg/football/en/Laws14_01.htm). FIFA. Archived from the original (http://www.fifa.com/flash/lotg/football/en/Laws14_01.htm) on 2007-09-13. . Retrieved 2007-10-14.
[55] "Referee's signals: advantage" (http://news.bbc.co.uk/sport1/hi/football/rules_and_equipment/4188646.stm). *BBC Sport*. BBC. . Retrieved 2011-03-04.
[56] IFAB. "Law 5: Referee: Advantage" (http://www.fifa.com/mm/document/affederation/generic/81/42/36/lawsofthegame_2010_11_e.pdf) (PDF). *Laws of the Game 2010/2011*. FIFA. p. 66. . Retrieved 2011-03-04.
[57] "Confederations" (http://www.fifa.com/aboutfifa/federation/confederations/index.html). FIFA. . Retrieved 2011-03-04.
[58] The number of competing teams has varied over the history of the competition. The most recent changed was in 1998, from 24 to 32.
[59] "The FIFA Calendar" (http://www.fifa.com/aboutfifa/calendar/events.html). FIFA. . Retrieved 2010-06-12.

[60] "Football Equipment and History" (http://www.olympic.org/football-equipment-and-history?tab=1). International Olympic Committee (IOC). . Retrieved 2011-03-04.
[61] "Football – An Olympic Sport since 1900" (http://replay.waybackmachine.org/20090601015157/http://www.olympic.org/uk/sports/programme/index_uk.asp?SportCode=FB). International Olympic Committee (IOC). Archived from the original (http://www.olympic.org/uk/sports/programme/index_uk.asp?SportCode=FB) on 2009-06-01. . Retrieved 2007-10-07.
[62] "Event Guide – Football" (http://olympics.sportinglife.com/olympics/story/0,23911,14986,00.html). *sportinglife*. 365 media group. . Retrieved 2011-03-05.
[63] "Organising Committee strengthens FIFA Club World Cup format" (http://www.fifa.com/clubworldcup/organisation/media/newsid=570740.html). FIFA. 2007-08-24. . Retrieved 2007-10-07.
[64] Fort, Rodney (September 2000). *Scottish Journal of Political Economy*. **47**. pp. 431–455. doi:10.1111/1467-9485.00172.
[65] "Estudiantes win Argentina Apertura title" (http://msn.foxsports.com/foxsoccer/latinamerica/story/Estudiantes-win-Argentina-Apertura-title). *FoxSports*. Associated Press. 2010-12-13. . "Under the system used in Argentina and most of Latin America, two season titles are awarded each year – the Apertura and Clausura."
[66] Hughes, Ian (2008-03-31). "Premier League conquering Europe" (http://news.bbc.co.uk/sport2/hi/football/europe/7321408.stm). *BBC Sport* (BBC). . Retrieved 2008-05-27.
[67] Taylor, Louise (2008-05-29). "Leading clubs losing out as players and agents cash in" (http://www.guardian.co.uk/football/2008/may/29/premierleague). *The Guardian* (London). . Retrieved 2008-11-28.
[68] Gregory, Patricia (2005-06-03). "How women's football battled for survival" (http://news.bbc.co.uk/sport1/hi/football/women/4607171.stm). *BBC sport* (BBC). . Retrieved 2010-02-19.
[69] Alexander, Shelley (2005-06-03). "Trail-blazers who pioneered women's football" (http://news.bbc.co.uk/sport1/hi/football/women/4603149.stm). *BBC sport* (BBC). . Retrieved 2010-02-19.
[70] "Tournaments: Women's World Cup" (http://www.fifa.com/tournaments/archive/tournament=103/awards/index.html). FIFA. . Retrieved 2011-03-11.

External links

- Federation Internationale de Football Association (FIFA) (http://www.fifa.com/)
- The Current Laws of the Game (LOTG) (http://www.fifa.com/worldfootball/lawsofthegame.html)
- The Rec.Sport.Soccer Statistics Foundation (RSSSF) (http://www.rsssf.com/)

Midfielder

In association football, a **midfielder** is a position.[1] Some midfielders play a more defensive role, while others blur the boundaries between midfielders and forwards.[2] The number of midfielders a team uses during a match may vary, depending on the team's formation and each individual player's role. The group of midfielders in a team is called **the midfield**.

More complete midfielders require a number of skills on top of fitness: they tackle, dribble, shoot and pass during any match. Most managers field at least one central midfielder with a marked task of breaking up opposition's attacks while the rest are more adept to creating goals or have equal responsibilities between attack and defence. At either side of the pitch a manager can field a right or left midfielder, who are used equally for both attack and defence, or a winger, a more attacking player used primarily for attack.

In essence, a good midfield must possess the ability to be combative while also being creative. A good striker without midfield support could lack attacking chances, while a defense likewise could be severely tested. Because they occupy the most influential parts of the pitch, midfielders are perhaps more likely to influence the outcome of a match than other positions,[3] especially if they have vision for a good pass or ability to score.

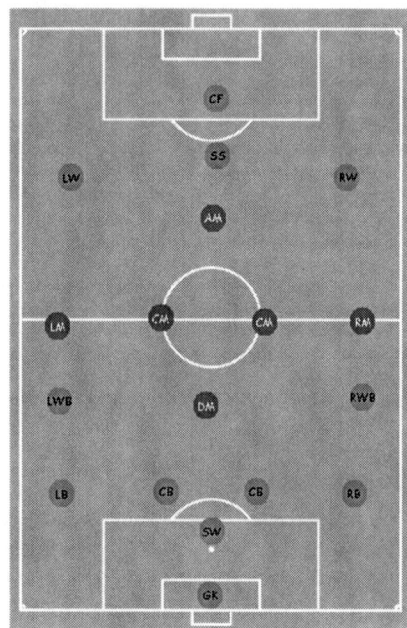

The Midfield in relation to the football positions

Midfielders typically expend the most energy during a match because of the distance they cover on a pitch, as at times they can be called back into defence, or required to attack with the strikers.[1]

Centre midfielder

Centre midfielders play several roles on the field of play, and are probably the most important in terms of setting up attacks. Their position enables them to have an all-round view of the match, and as most of the action takes place in and around their area of the pitch, midfielders often exert the greatest degree of control over how a match is played. This section of the field is often known as a team's "engine room", because great teams rarely succeed without skillful, commanding central midfielders.

Defensive midfielder

A **defensive midfielder** or a **holding midfielder** is often likened to an evolved version of the old-school sweeper.

The responsibilities of defensive midfielders usually include:

- Screening the defense by harrying and tackling the opposition teams' attackers and defenders.
- Covering the positions of full-backs, midfielders and even centre-backs as they advance into attack. This can be during open play or during set pieces such as free-kicks or corners.
- Retaining distribution nearer the defense. As passing square across the defense can be especially risky, the presence of the defensive midfielder just in front of defenders provides a relatively safer option going forward.
- **Directing** the distribution towards the flanks or further up front.
- Directing the opposition distribution to the flanks or deeper down their end, where they are less effective. Defensive midfielders are often pulled slightly towards the flank to deal with the threat of wingers cutting infield.

2 defensive midfielders are indicated in blue circles.

Although the duties of defensive midfielders are primarily defensive, some midfielders are deployed as ***deep-lying playmakers***, due to their ability to dictate tempo from a deep position with their passing. As they are not defensive specialists, they are typically supported by a more defensive holding midfielder.

Defensive midfielders require excellent positional sense, work rate, tackling ability, and anticipation (of player and ball movement) to excel. They also need to possess excellent passing skills and close control to hold the ball in midfield under sustained pressure. Most importantly, defensive midfielders require great stamina as they are the onfield players who cover the greatest distance during a professional football match. Deep-lying playmakers typically require a good first touch under opposition pressure and the ability to play long crossfield passes to attacking players further upfield.

The defensive midfielder position is also referred to in Brazilian Portuguese as *volante* and in South American Spanish as *volante de marca* (Spanish and Portuguese for "Rudder", or someone who gives direction), in Portugal as a *trinco* (meaning "lock"), in Mexico as "volante de contención" and in Russian as a *волнорез* (pronounced – vol-no-rez, meaning "breakwater"). Most Brazilian teams deploy at least one "volante" in their team, including the Brazilian national team who have fielded defensive midfielders, such as 1994 World Cup winning team captain Dunga.

Deep-lying playmaker

Some players prefer to set up an attack from a withdrawn position, and are often coined *deep-lying playmakers*, mainly because of their ability to spread play and dictate the game from a withdrawn position. Despite their deep role, they are not classed as defensive midfielders as tackling and defence are not the main function of their roles — they may have to be supported by a holding midfielder.

Deep-lying playmakers are typically given a moderate amount of defensive responsibilities, but are granted freedom positionally to dictate the play as it evolves as well as a license to attempt long, riskier balls to the forwards.

The essential attributes of a deep-lying playmaker include:

- Good **long passing** ability, to play balls towards forwards and wingers. Crossfield passes are typically attempted from deep when the opposing full back is drawn towards the middle and there is an open channel in the flank for

the on rushing winger.
- **Stamina**, to cover large distances in professional football. In the top football leagues, a midfielder covers upwards of 10 kilometres per game.
- **Short passing** ability. Although many deep-lying playmakers have natural talent and creativity, they are expected to play short simple passes when deep in their half to avoid the possibility of a counter-attack. They are however given some degree of freedom in playing long passes deep into opposition territory.
- **Creativity/Vision**. The deep-lying playmaker needs to spot openings and opportunities to build up play.
- A good and sure **first touch** to control the ball when receiving passes under sustained opposition pressure.

Attacking midfielder

An **attacking midfielder** is any midfielder who is stationed in a more advanced midfield position to assist goalscoring.[3] The attacking midfielder is an influential position and requires the player to possess good technical abilities, an eye for a pass, shooting, running, and dribbling skills.

Attacking midfielders are generally required to have:

- Excellent **technical** ability, including close control, passing, shooting and dribbling.
- **Creativity**, to anticipate passing opportunities for their fellow forwards.
- **Off-the-ball** intelligence, to anticipate passes from the midfield which create opportunities to score or to pass on to a forward.
- An understanding of the winger role. Due to tactical changes, central attacking midfielders are sometimes played on the wing, to accommodate other strikers or forwards.
- A secondary ability is finishing ability and composure.

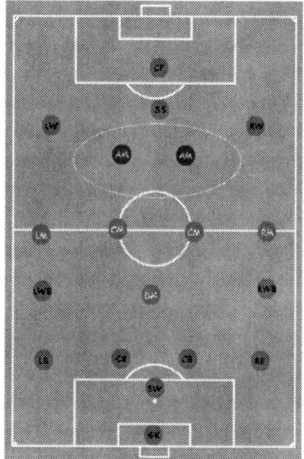

Two possible positions for an attacking midfielder are indicated in the yellow oval.

Playing in a very advanced central midfield role just behind the strikers is sometimes known as "playing in the hole", although this term can also be used to describe a deep lying forward, traditionally he/she is called a trequartista. This specialist midfielder's main role is to act as the offensive pivot of the team, to create goal-scoring opportunities for his team mates, and perhaps to score himself. He may be referred to as the playmaker.[2]

The attacking midfielder position is also referred to in Brazilian Portuguese as *meia'* or *'meia-atacante'* ("attacking midfielder" in English).

"Box-to-box" midfielder

The term 'box-to-box' player is often used to refer to the most dynamic all-round/complete midfielders, who provide both defensive and attacking prowess.[4] The most versatile of players, they typically possess exceptional stamina and are usually skilled at tackling, passing, shooting and also good at keeping possession.

Winger

A **winger** or **wide midfielder** is a midfielder located on the wing of the midfield. Traditionally, wingers were purely attacking players who hugged the touch line and were not expected to track back and defend. This began to change in the 1960s. In the 1966 World Cup, England manager Alf Ramsey did not select wingers from the quarter final onwards. This team was known as the "Wingless Wonders" and led to the modern 4–4–2 formation.[5][6]

This has led to most modern wide players having a more demanding role in the sense that they are expected to provide defensive cover for their full-backs and track back to repossess the ball, as well as provide skillful crosses for centre forwards and strikers.[7] Some forwards are able to operate as wingers behind a lone striker. In a three-man midfield, specialist wingers are sometimes deployed down the flanks alongside the central midfielder or playmaker.

Even more demanding is the role of wing-back, where the wide player is expected to provide both defence and attack.[8] As the role of winger can be classed as a forward or a midfielder, so this role blurs the divide between defender and midfielder.

A winger is an attacking midfielder who is stationed in a wide position near the touchlines.[7] Wingers such as Stanley Matthews or Jimmy Johnstone used to be classified as forwards in traditional W-shaped formations, and were formally known as "Outside Right" or "Outside Left", but as tactics evolved through the last 40 years, wingers have dropped to deeper field positions and are now usually classified as part of the midfield, usually in 4–4–2 or 4–5–1 formations (but while the team is on the attack, they tend to resemble 4–2–4 and 4–3–3 formations respectively).

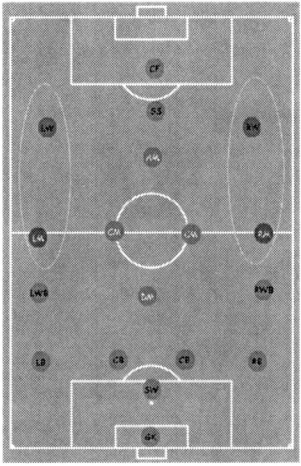

Wingers are indicated in red, while the 'wide men' (who play to the flanks of the centre midfielders) are indicated in blue.

The responsibilities of the winger include:

- Providing a "wide presence" as a passing option on the flank.
- To beat the opposing full-back either with skill or with speed.
- To read passes from the midfield that give them a clear crossing opportunity, when going wide, or that give them a clear scoring opportunity, when cutting inside towards goal.
- To double up on the opposition winger, particularly when he is being "double-marked" by both the team's full back and winger.

The stereotypical winger is fast, tricky and enjoys 'hugging' the touchline, that is, running downfield close to the touchline and delivering crosses. However, players with different attributes can thrive on the wing as well. Some wingers prefer to cut *infield* (as opposed to staying wide) and pose a threat as playmakers by playing diagonal passes to forwards or taking a shot at goal. Even players who are not considered quick, have been successfully fielded as wingers at club and international level for their ability to create play from the flank. Occasionally wingers are given a free role to roam across the front line and are relieved of defensive responsibilities.

The typical abilities of wingers include:

- Technical **skill** to beat a full-back in a one-to-one situation.
- **Pace**, to beat the full-back one-on-one.
- **Crossing** ability when out wide.
- Good **off-the-ball** ability when reading a pass from the midfield or from fellow attackers.
- Good **passing** ability and **composure**, to retain possession while in opposition territory.
- The modern winger should also be comfortable on either wing so as to adapt to quick tactical changes required by the coach.

Traditionally, right-footed players are played on the right wing and left-footed players on the left as a matter of familiarity and comfort. However, in the modern game, coaches usually demand wingers to be able to play on both flanks and to switch flanks during play regularly as a quick change of tactics. For instance, a right-footed winger who plays on the left flank is more comfortable cutting into the middle, which suits the styles of playmaker forwards who can cause a threat both by shooting from distance, dribbling towards goal, or sliding through passes to other forwards. Another advantage is that the winger can cut inside, towards the weaker foot of the full-back. Clubs such as Barcelona and Real Madrid often choose to play their wingers on the 'wrong' flank for this reason; Barcelona's Josep Guardiola puts left-footed Lionel Messi on the right and Pedro on the left, while Real Madrid's *entrenador* Jose Mourinho often plays Ángel di María on the right and Cristiano Ronaldo on the left. One of the foremost practitioners of playing from either flank was the German winger, Jürgen Grabowski, whose flexibility helped Germany to third place in the 1970 World Cup, and a championship in the 1974 World Cup.

Although wingers are a familiar part of football, the use of wingers is by no means universal. There are many successful football teams who operate without wingers. A famous example is AC Milan, who typically play in a narrow midfield diamond formation or in a Christmas tree formation (4–3–2–1), relying on full-backs to provide the necessary width down the wings.

See also

- Association football positions
- Formation
- Forward
- Outside forward
- Defender
- Goalkeeper
- Playmaker

References

[1] "Positions guide: Central midfield" (http://news.bbc.co.uk/sport1/hi/football/rules_and_equipment/4197190.stm). London: BBC Sport. 2005-09-01. . Retrieved 2008-06-21.
[2] "Football / Soccer Positions" (http://expertfootball.com/coaching/positions.php). Expert Football. . Retrieved 2008-06-21.
[3] "Positions in football" (http://www.talkfootball.co.uk/guides/positions_in_football.html). talkfootball.co.uk. . Retrieved 2008-06-21.
[4] "Box to box Bowyer" (http://news.bbc.co.uk/sport1/hi/football/1957308.stm). London: BBC Sport. 2002-04-29. . Retrieved 2008-06-21.
[5] Galvin, Robert. "Sir Alf Ramsey" (http://www.nationalfootballmuseum.com/pages/fame/Inductees/siralframsey.htm). nationalfootballmuseum.com. . Retrieved 2008-06-21.
[6] "Chelsea prayers fly to the wings" (http://www.fifa.com/tournaments/archive/tournament=107/edition=248388/news/newsid=103183.html). FIFA. 2006-03-05. . Retrieved 2008-06-25.
[7] "Positions guide: Wide midfield" (http://news.bbc.co.uk/sport1/hi/football/rules_and_equipment/4197228.stm). London: BBC Sport. 2005-09-01. . Retrieved 2008-06-21.
[8] "Positions guide: Wing-back" (http://news.bbc.co.uk/sport1/hi/football/rules_and_equipment/4197076.stm). London: BBC Sport. 2005-09-01. . Retrieved 2008-06-21.

Alpha Secondary School

Alpha Secondary	
Address	
4600 Parker Street Burnaby, British Columbia, V5C 3E2, Canada	
Information	
School number	4141005
School board	School District 41 Burnaby
Principal	Mr. R. Hall
Vice principal	Ms. D. Carr
Staff	61
School type	Public high school
Grades	8-12
Motto	*Where The Best Get Better*
Mascot	Aztecs (Previously Aardvark)
Team name	Aztecs
Colours	Blue and Gold
Founded	1950
Enrolment	993 (April 2009)
Homepage	http://alpha.sd41.bc.ca/

Alpha Secondary[1] is a public high school in Burnaby, British Columbia part of School District 41 Burnaby.

Academics

Alpha Secondary offers a broad range of educational programming, including Advanced Placement and Honours courses, as well as Ace-It programs. Students wishing to earn their professional certification as a hairstylist can enroll in the two year District Hairdressing Program which is located at Alpha. The Fitness Leadership Program is also at Alpha, which provides students with Douglas College credits, and BCRPA certification as weight training instructors. Alpha also has an integrated honours program for Grade 8 students called Discovery. In 2008, Alpha students earned over $410,000 in Scholarships.

Clubs and Councils

Students at Alpha are provided with a variety of leadership opportunities through their participation in over 30 clubs and councils. The main leadership groups are: Students' Council, Fine and Performing Arts Council, Grad Council, The Offence, and e-club. Other groups go beyond the school and organize events that improve both the local and global community. Through these groups, students organize school based events that contribute to the school culture.

Athletics

- 2003 Provincial AAA Boys Soccer - Placed 2nd
- 2004 Provincial AAA Boys Soccer Champions
- 2005 Provincial AAA Volleyball - Placed 3rd
- 2006 Provincial AAA Volleyball Champions
- 2007 Provincial AAA Volleyball - Placed 2nd

Alumni

- Ashley Leitao, a former top ten contestant on Canadian Idol, attended Alpha and graduated in 2004.
- Mike James (rugby), retired professional rugby player, former Team Canada captain
- Devon Sawa, Actor (Final Destination, Casper) (Class of 1998)
- Kea Wong, Actress (X-Men: The Last Stand, X2) (Class of 1996)
- Don Taylor, grad of 1983 currently working for Sportsnet, and the TEAM 1040
- Alfredo Valente, an Olympic Soccer player and Soccer player for the Vancouver Whitecaps FC, graduated from *Alpha in 1998.
- [[Joe Sakic]] Professional hockey player in the NHL, played for the Colorado Avalanche

References

[1] "For School Data, Source: BC Schools Book (http://www.bced.gov.bc.ca/schoolbook/)." *Province of British Columbia, Ministry of Education* January 16, 2006.

External links

- School website (http://alpha.sd41.bc.ca/)

School Reports - Ministry of Education

- Class Size (http://www.bced.gov.bc.ca/reports/pdfs/class_size/04141005.pdf)
- 2005/2006 Satisfaction Survey (http://www.bced.gov.bc.ca/reports/pdfs/sat_survey/2005/04141005.pdf)
- School Performance (http://www.bced.gov.bc.ca/reports/pdfs/school_perf/04141005.pdf)
- Skills Assessment (http://www.bced.gov.bc.ca/reports/pdfs/fsa/04141005.pdf)
</pre></pre>

Vancouver Whitecaps (1986–2010)

Full name	Vancouver Whitecaps FC
Nickname(s)	'Caps
Founded	1986 as Vancouver 86ers[1]
Dissolved	2010 (MLS 2011)
Ground	Swangard Stadium Burnaby, British Columbia (Capacity: 5,288)
Owner	Greg Kerfoot
Head Coach	Teitur Thordarson
League	USSF Division 2 Professional League
2010	Regular Season: 2nd, NASL Overall: 5th Playoffs: Semifinals
Website	Club home page [2]

Home colours Away colours

Vancouver Whitecaps FC was a Canadian professional soccer club based in Vancouver, British Columbia. Founded in 1986, the team played its final year in the second tier of the United States soccer pyramid in the NASL Conference of the USSF Division 2 Professional League coached by Teitur Thordarson. The team played its home games at Swangard Stadium in nearby Burnaby, British Columbia, where they have played since 2003. The team's colours are blue and white.

On March 19, 2009, an ownership group led by **Vancouver Whitecaps FC** principal Greg Kerfoot was granted a Major League Soccer expansion franchise set to begin play in 2011 at Vancouver's Empire Field, and then once renovations are complete in BC Place Stadium.

In addition to its men's side the Whitecaps also field a women's team in the USL W-League, two developmental teams (Vancouver Whitecaps Residency, in the USL Premier Development League, and the Whitecaps FC Prospects, in the Pacific Coast Soccer League), and four youth teams in the USL Super Y-League (Coastal WFC, Mountain WFC, Surrey WFC and Okanagan WFC) ranging in age from U13 to U17 for both boys and girls.[2]

The team was previously known as the **Vancouver 86ers** of both the Canadian Soccer League and later the A-League. The franchise later played in several second tier leagues in North America.

History

Vancouver 86ers

In 1986, a professional soccer team was again launched in Vancouver, the Vancouver 86ers—so named because of both the year of the team's founding and to commemorate the year Vancouver was founded (1886). The 86ers played in the Canadian Soccer League (CSL) winning 4 straight CSL Championships (1988–1991) and 5 consecutive CSL regular-season first-place finishes (1988–92). In 1990, the Vancouver 86ers captured the North American Club Championship after defeating the Maryland Bays 3–2 in the final

Vancouver 86ers

played in Burnaby. The game was played between the champions of the Canadian Soccer League and the champions of the American Professional Soccer League (APSL). Vancouver played in the CSL from its inception in 1987 until the league folded in 1992, and then moved over to the APSL in 1993 which was later absorbed into the USL hierarchy of leagues in 1997 becoming the A-League, later renamed the USL.

In 1988–1989, the team, coached by Bob Lenarduzzi, set a North American professional sports record by playing 46 consecutive games without a loss.[4]

Vancouver Whitecaps (USL)

In 2001, the team began to use the old Vancouver Whitecaps moniker (signifying both the 'white caps' of the nearby mountains, and the waves of the Pacific Ocean). The Whitecaps currently practise on the new turf field at Simon Fraser University.

In 2003, the name was again changed, albeit only slightly, to Whitecaps FC, which encompasses the men's, women's, and youth development teams within the organization. At this time, the Whitecaps logo changed slightly in colour (the light teal-green was replaced with a brighter blue) and the word "Vancouver" was dropped from the image.

Vancouver Whitecaps USL

In 2006, the Whitecaps organization won an unprecedented double-championship, claiming both the United Soccer Leagues First Division championship trophy, defeating the host Rochester Rhinos 3–0 at PAETEC Park, and winning the W-League women's trophy. The men's team also won the Nation's Cup, a new tournament established by their club as a way to feature the Whitecaps playing against international competition. The 2006 Nation's Cup tournament featured the Chinese and Indian U-20 National teams and Championship Welsh club Cardiff City F.C. (the "Bluebirds"). The gradually added the "Vancouver" back into their name, changing it officially to "Vancouver Whitecaps FC".

The following season, the Whitecaps signed a deal to play an exhibition match against the Los Angeles Galaxy, which featured international David Beckham, and promoted Director of Soccer Operations Bob Lenarduzzi to team president.

October 12, 2008, they claimed their second United Soccer Leagues First Division championship with a 2–1 victory over the Puerto Rico Islanders. Charles Gbeke scored twice with his head in the second half to help secure the title. In 2009, they placed 7th in the league and were eliminated in the final by the Montreal Impact on a 6–3 aggregate.[3]

In November 2009 the Whitecaps, along with several other teams, announced their intent to leave the USL First Division to become the co-founders of a new North American Soccer League, which was to begin play in 2010.[4] [5] On 7 January the U.S.S.F. announced that neither the USL nor the NASL would be permitted to have a second division league,[6] and the USSF would administer a league where the NASL and USL are conferences within the league.[7]

On 24 November 2009 it was announced that Paul Barber, the former Executive Director of Tottenham Hotspur, will become the Chief Executive Operations director of the Caps.[8]

Whitecaps played a 30-match regular season, with 15 home games and a 15 games away in the United States Soccer Federation Division 2 Professional League.[9]

The Whitecaps and Major League Soccer

On July 24, 2008, the MLS announced they were seeking to add two expansion franchises for the 2011 season.[10] One day later, the Whitecaps officially announced that they were pursuing one of the two expansion slots. The Whitecaps also announced that local sports icon Steve Nash will join the Whitecaps ownership team.[11]

"There is no doubt the market for professional soccer exists in Vancouver, as we saw last November when nearly 50,000 fans attended the exhibition match between the Los Angeles Galaxy and the Whitecaps, " MLS commissioner Don Garber said.[12]

Vancouver's bid was officially submitted on October 15, 2008, along with bids from 6 other cities.[13] Whitecaps representatives Greg Kerfoot and Jeff Mallett met with MLS officials on November 21, 2008 to go over their bid. Don Garber, who was previously involved in National Football League expansion, described the bid presentation as, "one of the best I've ever seen."[14] Garber and MLS president Mark Abbott were in Vancouver on December 7, 2008 to tour BC Place Stadium and learn about the proposed renovations, which are scheduled to be completed in time for the 2011 MLS season.[15]

Vancouver was officially named an MLS expansion city on March 18, 2009, and joined the league in 2011. They began their inaugural MLS season at Empire Field, a temporary stadium built at the former site of Empire Stadium, and will move into BC Place Stadium[16] [17] [18] [19] once renovations to the stadium are complete.

Players

Final roster

as of October 29, 2010[20]

Note: Flags indicate national team as has been defined under FIFA eligibility rules. Players may hold more than one non-FIFA nationality.

No.	Position	Player
1	GK	Jay Nolly
3	DF	Luca Bellisomo
6	MF	Terry Dunfield
8	DF	Wes Knight
9	MF	Davide Chiumiento
11	FW	Ridge Mobulu
12	MF	Russell Teibert
14	DF	Greg Janicki
15	MF	Philippe Davies
16	MF	Kyle Porter
20	MF	Ethan Gage

No.	Position	Player
23	DF	Blake Wagner
24	MF	Alexandre Morfaw
25	FW	Cody Arnoux
26	FW	Alex Semenets
28	MF	Gershon Koffie
29	MF	Nizar Khalfan
31	GK	Simon Thomas
33	DF	Willis Forko
39	FW	Cornelius Stewart
55	DF	Mouloud Akloul
	MF	Bedri Gashi

Out on loan

Note: Flags indicate national team as has been defined under FIFA eligibility rules. Players may hold more than one non-FIFA nationality.

No.	Position	Player
	DF	Alain Rochat *(at FC Zürich)*[21]

Notable former players

- Nicholas Addlery
- Nelson Akwari
- Vicente Arze
- Geoff Aunger
- Tyrell Burgess
- Tony Caig
- Adrian Cann
- Carlo Corazzin
- Jeff Clarke
- Nick Dasovic
- Charles Gbeke
- Joey Gjertsen

- Richard Goddard
- Bruce Grobbelaar
- Marcus Haber
- Kevin Harmse
- Takashi Hirano
- Lars Hirschfeld
- Kevin Holness
- Jason Jordan
- Steve Kindel
- Steve Klein
- Landon Ling
- Shaun Lowther

- Geordie Lyall
- Lyle Martin
- Sita-Taty Matondo
- Josué Mayard
- Jonathan McDonald
- Dale Mitchell
- Domenic Mobilio
- Martin Nash
- Matt Nelson
- Anthony Noreiga
- Marco Reda

- Lutz Pfannenstiel
- Eduardo Sebrango
- Ryan Suarez
- Johnny Sulentic
- David Testo
- Niall Thompson
- Rick Titus
- Ansu Toure
- Kénold Versailles
- Chris Williams
- Davide Xausa

- See also: All-time Vancouver Whitecaps roster

Staff

Management

- Greg Kerfoot *Owner*
- Bob Lenarduzzi *President*
- Paul Barber *Chief Executive Officer*
- Rachel Lewis *Chief Operating Officer*
- Dave Irvine *Manager of Technical Programs*
- Tom Soehn *Director of Soccer Operations*
- Chris Murphy *Director of Professional Development*
- Dan Lenarduzzi *Director of Youth Development*

Sports

- Teitur Thordarson *Head Coach*
- Colin Miller *Assistant Coach*
- Mike Salmon *Goalkeeping Coach*

Medical

- Graeme Poole *Physiotherapist*
- Chris Franks *Physiotherapist*
- Al Ezaki *Athletic Therapist*
- Dr. Bob McCormack *Team Physician*
- Dr. Jim Bovard *Team Physician*
- Steve Ramsbottom *Strength & Conditioning Specialist*
- Darren Woloshen *Equipment Manager*

Year-by-Year

Year	Division	League	Regular Season	Playoffs	Voyageurs Cup
1987		CSL	2nd, Western	Semifinals	N/A
1988		CSL	1st, Western	Champion	N/A
1989		CSL	1st, Western	Champion	N/A
1990		CSL	1st, Western	Champion	N/A
1991		CSL	1st	Champion	N/A
1992		CSL	1st	Final	N/A
1993		APSL	1st	Semifinals	N/A
1994		APSL	6th	*Did not qualify*	N/A
1995	2	A-League	3rd	Semifinals	N/A
1996	2	A-League	5th	*Did not qualify*	N/A
1997	2	USISL A-League	3rd, Pacific	Conference Finals	N/A
1998	2	USISL A-League	4th, Pacific	Conference Quarterfinals	N/A
1999	2	USL A-League	2nd, Pacific	Conference Quarterfinals	N/A
2000	2	USL A-League	3rd, Pacific	Conference Semifinals	N/A
2001	2	USL A-League	1st, Western	Semifinals	N/A

Vancouver Whitecaps (1986–2010)

2002	2	USL A-League	3rd, Pacific	Conference Finals	3rd
2003	2	USL A-League	2nd, Pacific	Division Finals	3rd
2004	2	USL A-League	2nd, Western	Semifinals	4th
2005	2	USL First Division	3rd	Quarterfinals	2nd
2006	2	USL First Division	4th	Champion	3rd
2007	2	USL First Division	7th	Quarterfinals	2nd
2008	2	USL First Division	2nd	Champion	3rd
2009	2	USL First Division	7th	Final	2nd
2010	2	USSF Division 2	2nd, NASL (5th)	Semifinals	2nd

Honours

Domestic

Canadian Soccer League
- **Canadian Soccer League Championship**
  - Winners (4): 1988, 1989, 1990, 1991
  - Runners-up (1): 1992
- **Canadian Soccer League Regular Season Champion**
  - Winners (5): 1988, 1989, 1990, 1991, 1992
- **Canadian Championship**
  - Runners up (2): *2009, 2010*

USL First Division
- **USL First Division Championship**
  - Winners (2): 2006, 2008
  - Runners-up (1): 2009
- **Commissioner's Cup**
  - Winners (1): 1993
  - Runners-up (1): 2008
- **Voyageurs Cup**
  - Runners-up (2): 2005, 2007
- **Cascadia Cup**
  - Winners (3): 2004, 2005, 2008
  - Runners-up (3): 2006, 2007, 2009

International

- **North American Club Championship**
  - Winners (1): 1990
- **Nations Cup**
  - Winners (1): 2006

Head coaches

- Bob Lenarduzzi (1988–1989)
- Bob Lilley (2007)
- Teitur Thordarson (2008–2010)

Stadia

- Swangard Stadium; Burnaby, British Columbia (2003–2010)

Proposed new stadium

The City of Vancouver is currently considering a proposal for Whitecaps Waterfront Stadium, a new stadium to be built over the railway tracks east of Waterfront Station on Burrard Inlet. This 16,000 seat stadium would replace Swangard Stadium as the home field for the USL's Vancouver Whitecaps. There is a fair degree of controversy with regards to this location; a Vancouver council session to debate the issue was extended to four nights to allow public input. Detractors view the proposed stadium as an incongruous addition to nearby historic Gastown that would block waterfront access and promote piecemeal development of the area. Proponents of the development feel that the stadium will attract new business to the downtown and Gastown areas, particularly since the soccer team tends to attract a family-oriented audience.

On July 11, 2006, Vancouver City Council voted unanimously to proceed with the stadium project, so long as the Whitecaps could meet certain conditions regarding land use. On January 22, 2007, the Whitecaps filed a new proposal shifting the proposed site for the stadium project to the current location of the SeaBus terminal, a short distance northwest of the previous site.

With the Whitecaps moving up to MLS, the franchise has signed to initially play at Empire Field, and then BC Place Stadium from 2011 to at least 2015. It is hoped that the new facility will be completed by the 2016 MLS season.

Club culture

Mascot

The Whitecaps' mascot is named Winger. He is a bird who wears a Whitecaps jersey and carries a large drum to encourage the crowd. He often uses signs to get fans in the grandstands to cheer.

Winger is the mascot of the Vancouver Whitecaps

Fans

The Southsiders in the supporters section of Swangard Stadium

The Whitecaps have an independent supporters group known as the *Southsiders*.[22] [23] Founded in 1999, the group is named for their preferred seating area in the south end of Swangard Stadium. The Southsiders, once described as a "rabid supporters group",[24] identify themselves as Canada's oldest supporters association for professional domestic association football.

The group originally called themselves "The Carlsberg Crew," named for the beer company that sponsored Swangard's beer garden. The name was changed to "The Canterbury Chorus" for the subsequent season, as the beer sponsorship had changed between seasons. To avoid changing names every time the sponsor changed, the group chose the name "The Southsiders".[25]

Rival clubs

The Vancouver Whitecaps have two historic rivals, the Pacific Northwest Portland Timbers and Seattle Sounders. These three teams competed in the yearly Cascadia Cup through 2008. In 2009, the Cup involved only the Whitecaps and Timbers because the Sounders were replaced by an MLS team of the same name.

The Whitecaps also compete on a yearly basis with the Montreal Impact and Toronto FC for the Nutrilite Canadian Championship. The winner of this series advances to the CONCACAF Champions League.

References

[1] (http://www.whitecapsfc.com/archive/feature02270901.aspx)
[2] http://www.whitecapsfc.com/youth/teams/super_y_affiliates/
[3] "Montreal wins USL-1 title" (http://www.uslsoccer.com/home/375255.html). www.uslsoccer.com. 2009-10-17. . Retrieved 2010-01-09.
[4] USL outcasts set to launch new league in 2010 (http://www.soccerbyives.net/soccer_by_ives/2009/11/usl-outcasts-set-to-launch-new-league-in-2010.html)
[5] CBC Sports: Whitecaps, Impact to form breakaway league. (http://www.cbc.ca/sports/soccer/story/2009/11/10/sp-usl-new-league.html)
[6] "US Soccer Federation To Oversee Combined NASL/USL League" (http://www.goal.com/en-us/news/66/united-states/2010/01/07/1731779/us-soccer-federation-to-oversee-combined-naslusl-league). Goal.com. 2010-01-07. . Retrieved 2010-01-08.
[7] "Impact, Whitecaps join new league" (http://www.torontosun.com/sports/soccer/2010/01/07/12384771-qmi.html). Toronto Sun. 2010-01-07. . Retrieved 2010-01-08.
[8] Whitecaps appoint CEO from EPL club (http://www.whitecapsfc.com/archive/feature11240902.aspx)
[9] 2010 regular season announced (http://www.whitecapsfc.com/archive/feature02081002.aspx)

[10] Major League Soccer: News: Article (http://web.mlsnet.com/news/mls_news.jsp?ymd=20080724&content_id=175344&vkey=pr_mls&fext=.jsp)
[11] 'Caps pursue franchise in MLS (http://www.whitecapsfc.com/archive/feature07250801.aspx)
[12] http://web.mlsnet.com/news/mls_news.jsp?16&content_id=158409&vkey=pr_mls&fext=.jsp
[13] "MLS News and Notes" (http://www.nj.com/sports/njsports/index.ssf/2008/11/mls_news_and_notes.html). The Star-Ledger. 2008-11-21. .
[14] "MLS expansion fee won't scare away Whitecaps" (http://www.canada.com/vancouversun/news/sports/story.html?id=a0af2cc5-5873-45db-a550-724e0daac136). The Vancouver Sun. 2008-11-25. .
[15] "MLS bosses tour BC Place" (http://www.vancouversun.com/Sports/bosses+tour+Place/1060574/story.html). The Vancouver Sun. 2008-12-11. .
[16] "MLS expected to announce Vancouver expansion team" (http://www.cbc.ca/sports/soccer/story/2009/03/17/sp-whitecaps-expansion.html). CBC News. 2009-03-17. .
[17] "Whitecaps to announce they will join MLS in 2011" (http://www.vancouversun.com/Sports/Whitecaps+expected+announce+they+will+join+2011/1398865/story.html). The Vancouver Sun. 2009-03-17. .
[18] "Whitecaps to announce MLS franchise secured" (http://www.canada.com/Sports/Whitecaps+announce+franchise+secured/1399199/story.html). Canwest News Service. 2009-03-17. .
[19] MLS awards Vancouver team for 2011 (http://www.whitecapsfc.com/archive/feature03180901.aspx)
[20] http://www.whitecapsfc.com/men/roster/default.aspx
[21] http://www.whitecapsfc.com/archive/feature08171002.aspx
[22] The Official Supporters Group of The Vancouver Whitecaps (USSF D2) (http://www.whitecapsfc.com/matchday/supporters/)
[23] Vancouver Southsiders (http://www.vancouversouthsiders.com)
[24] Steedman, Scott (September 10, 2010). "Taking the ball" (http://www.vancourier.com/sports/Taking+ball/3505841/story.html). *Vancouver Courier.* . Retrieved September 20, 2010.
[25] The Southsiders Official Homepage. (http://www.vancouversouthsiders.ca/history.html/,) Retrieved on July 22, 2010.

External links

- Vancouver Whitecaps Official Site (http://www.whitecapsfc.com)
- Mountain WFC (http://www.mountainwfc.ca/)
- Surrey WFC (http://www.surreywfc.com/)
- Coastal WFC (http://www.coastalwfc.com/)

Vancouver Metro Soccer League

Countries	Canada
Confederation	Canadian Soccer Association
Founded	1973, as the British Columbia Senior Soccer League
Divisions	3 Men's Divisions, 3 Masters Divisions, U-21
Number of teams	12 teams in premier divisions
Levels on pyramid	5
Promotion to	None
Relegation to	None
Current champions	Surrey United Firefighters (2009-10)
Most championships	Firefighters FC (7 league championships), Columbus Clan FC (6 Imperial Cups)
Website	http://www.vmslsoccer.com/

The Vancouver Metro Soccer League (**VMSL**) is a soccer league for men operating in British Columbia, primarily in the Lower Mainland area.

History

The league is an amateur league, and does not compete against or promote teams to the Canadian Soccer Pyramid. The league is officially considered to be one-tier below the Pacific Coast Soccer League, although because the PCSL is registered as an American league and both provide comparable play, the VMSL is often seen as providing the same level of competition.

The league has been home to several former USL First Division players, including Johnny Sulentic (Croatia SC), Alfredo Valente (Coquitlam Metro-Ford), David Morris (Pegasus FC), Jason Jordan (RCIU Legends), Jeff Clarke (Surrey United), Steve Kindel (Columbus Clan FC) and Ivor Evans (Richmond FC Olympics), who generally play in this league while free agents.

This league has produced several British Columbia Soccer Association Provincial Cup Champions, including seven of the last ten champions. In 2007, the league also produced a runner-up to the Open Canada Cup in Columbus Clan FC.

2010-11 Teams

[1]

- Akal FC 'A' (promoted from division 1A)
- Columbus FC
- Coquitlam Metro-Ford Wolves 'A'
- Croatia SC
- Delta United
- ICSF Inter 'A'
- ICST Pegasus 'A'
- Punjab Hurricanes (promoted from division 1B)
- Richmond FC Hibernians

Vancouver Metro Soccer League

- Sapperton Rovers 'A'
- Serbian White Eagles (promoted from division 1A)
- Surrey United Firefighters
- West Van FC 'A'
- Westside FC 'A'

Imperial Cup

Teams in the VMSL play for the Imperial Cup, which has been contested since 1913.

Imperial Cup Champions:

- 1913 Thistle FC
- 1914 No Competition
- 1915 No Competition
- 1916 No Competition
- 1917 No Competition
- 1918 No Competition
- 1919 No Competition
- 1920 Thistle FC
- 1921 Wallace FC
- 1922 South Hill Army & Navy
- 1923 South Hill Army & Navy
- 1924 North Van Elks FC
- 1925 St. Andrew's FC
- 1926 Sapperton FC
- 1927 No Competition
- 1928 No Competition
- 1929 No Competition
- 1930 No Competition
- 1931 No Competition
- 1932 No Competition
- 1933 No Competition
- 1934 Art Monument FC
- 1935 Unknown
- 1936 Unknown
- 1937 St. Regis FC
- 1938 Excelsior Lumber
- 1939 Unknown
- 1940 Kerrisdale FC
- 1941 Unknown
- 1942 Richmond FC
- 1943 Unknown
- 1944 Army FC
- 1945 Norvan FC
- 1946 Vancouver United
- 1947 Collingwood FC
- 1948 Norquay FC
- 1949 Rainier Hotel FC

Vancouver Metro Soccer League

- 1950 South Hill FC and James Bldrs.
- 1951 Varsity FC
- 1952 A. N. & AF Unit #100
- 1953 Vancouver Pilseners
- 1954 Vancouver Pilseners
- 1955 Dubbell Wear FC
- 1956 Royal Oaks FC
- 1957 Capilanos FC
- 1958 Capilanos FC
- 1959 Wallace FC
- 1960 Vancouver Firefighters
- 1961 Vancouver Firefighters
- 1962 Royal Oaks FC
- 1963 University of BC
- 1964 Mount Pleasant Legion
- 1965 Vancouver Friuli
- 1966 North Shore United
- 1967 Lobbans FC
- 1968 Royal Oaks FC
- 1969 Glenavon FC and Lobbans
- 1970 Glenavon FC
- 1971 Lobbans FC
- 1972 Royal Oak Astors
- 1973 Vancouver Firefighters
- 1974 North Shore United
- 1975 North Shore Paul's
- 1976 Unknown
- 1977 Italian Canadian Columbus
- 1978 Columbus FC
- 1979 Columbus Umberto
- 1980 Columbus Umberto
- 1981 Cliff Avenue United
- 1982 Vancouver Firefighters
- 1983 Vancouver Firefighters
- 1984 Discovery '84 FC
- 1985 Norvan ANAF #45 FC
- 1986 Norvan ANAF #45 FC
- 1987 Queen's Park Rangers
- 1988 Dartmen FC
- 1989 West Van Trollers
- 1990 Burnaby Lake Clubhouse
- 1991 Vancouver Firefighters
- 1992 Club Ireland FC
- 1993 Club Ireland FC
- 1994 Westside Rino
- 1995 Wesburn
- 1996 Croatia SC

- 1997 Croatia SC
- 1998 Croatia SC
- 1999 Indo-Canadians
- 2000 Westside FC 'A'
- 2001 ICSF Inter
- 2002 Westside Rino
- 2003 Westside Rino
- 2004 Pegasus FC
- 2005 Croatia SC
- 2006 Columbus-Clan FC
- 2007 Columbus-Clan FC
- 2008 Surrey United
- 2009 West Van FC
- 2010 Surrey United Firefighters

Premier Division Champions

- 1982–83 Firefighters "A"
- 1983–84 Firefighters "A"
- 1984–85 Firefighters "A"
- 1985–86 Firefighters "A"
- 1986–87 Firefighters "A"
- 1987–88 Firefighters "A"
- 1988–89 Metro-Ford Wolves
- 1989–90 Norvan SC
- 1990–91 Norvan SC
- 1991–92 Metro-Ford Wolves
- 1992–93 Metro-Ford Wolves
- 1993–94 Westside Rino
- 1994–95 North Shore Pegasus
- 1995–96 North Shore Pegasus
- 1996–97 Sapperton Rovers
- 1997–98 Firefighters "A"
- 1998–99 Westside FC "A"
- 1999–00 Westside FC "A"
- 2000–01 Rino's Westside
- 2001–02 Surrey United
- 2002–03 Westside Rino
- 2003–04 Surrey United
- 2004–05 ICSF Inter
- 2005–06 Surrey United
- 2006–07 ICSF Inter
- 2007–08 Sporting Club of Vancouver
- 2008–09 West Van FC

References

[1] VMSL - PREMIER DIVISION (http://www.vmslsoccer.com/prem_stand.html)

External links

- Official site (http://www.vmslsoccer.com/)

Canada men's national under-20 soccer team

Nickname(s)	The Canucks, The Maple Leafs, Les Rouges (*The Reds*)
Association	Canadian Soccer Association
Confederation	CONCACAF (North America)
Head coach	Valerio Gazzola
Most caps	David Edgar (27)
Top scorer	Iain Hume (7)
FIFA code	CAN

Home colours   Away colours

First international

Mexico 4–2 Canada
(Vancouver, Canada; August 16, 1977)

Biggest win

Canada 9–0 Dominican Republic
(Tegucigalpa, Honduras; November 26, 1978)

Biggest defeat

United States 5–0 Canada
(Sunrise, Florida, USA; December 18, 2010)
Niger 6–1 Canada
(Niamey, Niger; December 8, 2005)
Cameroon 5–0 Canada
(Niamey, Niger; December 6, 2005)

CONCACAF U-20 Championship

Appearances	18 (*First in 1973*)
Best result	Winners, (1986 and 1996)

Canada U-20 men's national soccer team, also known as Canada Under-20s or Canada U-20s, is the youth club for national soccer in Canada. It plays a large role in the development of Canadian soccer, and is considered to be the feeder team for the Canada men's national soccer team. The team has qualified for 8 out of 16 FIFA U-20 World Cups and five of the last six, and their best result came in 2003 where they reached the Quarter-finals.

The team also competes in the CONCACAF U20 Tournament, and many of its members are former FIFA U-17 World Cup participants. Will Johnson was among the veterans of the side to take part in the 2008 CONCACAF

Olympic qualifying tournament.

Team history

1976–1996

Canada's Under-20 soccer team was created in 1976 as Canada's response to the newly created World youth Championship. The team failed to qualify for the inaugural tournament in 1977 in Tunisia, but they qualified for the following tournament two years later in Japan. They finished last in their group with two points, but they did manage to defeat Portugal 3–1. The next time the team qualified for a World youth Championship was in 1985, in the USSR, again they came last in their group with only one point. In the 1987 WYC in Chile, Canada's Under-20 soccer team put up a good effort scoring four goals, and tying Italy, however they still did not manage to get out of the group stage.

1997–2004

In 1997, after failing to qualify for four World Youth Championships (as the event was known until 2005) in a row, Canada made it past the group stage. The team progressed to the second round ater a 2–1 win against Hungary in which a young Dwayne De Rosario scored a goal. They lost the round of 16 game against Spain 2–0.

After missing the tournament in 1999, Canada qualified for Argentina 2001 after winning the qualifying tournament based on home soil in Vancouver, British Columbia. At the finals, they finished last and were eliminated from a group including Brazil, Germany and Iraq.

Canada once again appeared in the 2003 FIFA World Youth Championship in United Arab Emirates. They qualified to the round of 16 where they blanked Burkina Faso 1–0, and in a rematch against 1997 conquerors Spain, Canada lost in the quarter finals. Iain Hume scored three goals for Canada including a direct free kick against Spain while Atiba Hutchinson was an impressive performer in midfield.

2005–Present

In the 2005 FIFA World Youth Championships in the Netherlands, Canada were eliminated in the group stage after tying once and losing twice. One bright side of the tournament was Jaime Peters' and Marcel De Jong's goals.

In the build-up to the 2007 FIFA U-20 World Cup, as the tournament came to be known, Canada's defeated Brazil in the first game of a three game series, winning 2- in front of 14 000+ at Commonwealth Stadium in Edmonton on May 19, 2006. David Edgar and Will Johnson scored and Stephen Lumley made goal-line clearance to preserve Canada's first win over a Brazilian men's team at any level. Canada lost the remaining two matches 3–1. Despite an impressive run in friendlies leading up to the competition, Canada went winless in first round play without scoring a goal on home soil.

Current U-20 national team members

Players called to Florida training camp in December 2010 and for matches against the USA in Boca Raton. [1]

Head coach: Valerio Gazzola

No.	Pos.	Player	DoB/Age	Caps	Club
	GK	Julien Latendresse-Lévesque	February 27, 1991	3	FC Energie Cottbus
	GK	Roberto Stillo	March 15, 1991	4	Genoa
	DF	Sven Arapovic	January 23, 1991	1	Toronto Croatia
	DF	Derrick Bassi	February 29, 1992	2	Vancouver Whitecaps Residency
	DF	Doneil Henry	April 20, 1993	2	Toronto FC
	DF	Roger Thompson	December 19, 1991	2	University of Cincinnati
	DF	Ashtone Morgan	February 9, 1991	2	Toronto FC Academy
	DF	Chris Suta	November 7, 1991	1	University of Detroit Mercy
	DF	Vince Caminiti	August 4, 1991	0	AEK London FC
	DF	Sean Hart	June 25, 1991	2	Schulz Academy
	MF	Jaineil Hoilett	November 5, 1992	3	Mainz 05
	MF	Ethan Gage	May 8, 1991	8	Reading F.C.
	MF	Jonathan Osorio	December 6, 1991	2	Clarkson Sheridan
	MF	Matt Stinson	September 9, 1992	3	Toronto FC
	MF	Kevin Cobby	March 31, 1992	2	Vancouver Whitecaps Residency
	MF	Oscar Cordon	January 18, 1993	0	Toronto FC
	FW	Nicholas Lindsay	September 3, 1992	2	Toronto FC
	FW	Jerome Baker	August 9, 1991	2	FC Edmonton
	FW	Niall Cousens	February 25, 1991	2	Slavia Praha
	FW	Erik Grigore	October 25, 1991	0	North York Astros
	FW	Massimo Mirabelli	October 21, 1991	1	Portugal FC

Recent call-ups

All call-ups updated to August 17, 2010. [2] [3]

No.	Pos.	Player	DoB/Age	Caps	Club
	GK	Jordan Santiago	April 3, 1991	0	Cardiff City
	DF	Francesco Augustin	February 3, 1992	1	Montreal Impact Academy
	DF	James Chalk	September 2, 1992	1	PSG
	DF	Serge Dinkota	April 22, 1991	0	Montreal Impact Academy
	DF	Gino Mauro	May 6, 1991	1	Derthona F.B.C. 1908
	DF	Amine Meftouh	January 4, 1992	1	Montreal Impact Academy
	DF	Dominic Roberts		0	Southern New Hampshire University
	DF	Daniel Di Biagio	December 1, 1991	0	Winthrop University
	MF	Liam Connon	March 28, 1991	1	Ross County
	MF	Darren Jones	October 16, 1991	1	Western Michigan Broncos
	MF	Andrew Kliment	June 4, 1991	0	FK Bohemians Praha
	MF	Justin Maheu	January 23, 1991	1	Fortuna Düsseldorf

MF	Russell Teibert	December 22, 1992	1		Vancouver Whitecaps
MF	Sergio Camargo	August 16, 1994	0		Toronto FC Academy
MF	Mahir Hadžirešić	September 12, 1991	0		FK Mladá Boleslav
MF	Marco Rodriguez	July 1, 1992	0		Club Atlético Platense
FW	Joseph Costouros	March 31, 1991	0		Leixões
FW	Liam Kelly	September 20, 1991	1		Creighton University
FW	Jelani Smith	January 1, 1991	0		FCGU Eagles Joshua Mathis
FW	Abdoulaye Sylla	December 10, 1992	1		FC Metz

Staff

- Head Coach ... **Valerio Gazzola**
- Assistant Coach ... **Mark Watson**
- Goalkeeper coach ... **Djamel Laarabi**
- Athletic Therapist ... **Jared Postance**
- Athletic Therapist ... **Dave Foley**
- Manager ... **Morgan Quarry**

Notable former players

- Andres Arango
- Robbie Aristodemo
- Richard Asante
- Nana Attakora-Gyan
- Asmir Begović
- Ivan Belfiore
- Wyn Belotte
- Brandon Bonifacio
- Jeff Cambridge
- Maycoll Cañizalez
- Gordon Chin
- Christopher Chueden
- Pat Cubellis
- Julian de Guzman
- Pasquale De Luca
- Jason DiTullio
- Srdjan Djekanovic
- Terry Dunfield
- Randy Edwini-Bonsu
- Chris Franks
- David Fronimadis
- Sean Fraser
- Nick Gilbert
- Elliott Godfrey
- Gerry Gray
- Ryan Gyaki
- Marcus Haber
- Pat Harrington
- Winston Marshall
- Sita-Taty Matondo
- Bruce Miller
- Tristan Murray
- Miles O'Connor
- Riley O'Neill
- Giuliano Oliveiro
- Andrew Olivieri
- Rosario Ongaro
- Brad Parker
- Tony Pignatiello
- Igor Pisanjuk
- Rocco Placentino
- Randy Ragan
- Antonio Ribeiro
- Marco Rizi
- Bryan Rosenfeld
- Peter Sarantopoulos
- Jeremy Sheperd
- Eddy Sidra
- Peter Sloly
- Ive Sulentic
- Mike Sweeney
- Justin Thompson
- Niall Thompson
- Guido Titotto
- Chris Turner
- Igor Vrablic

- Tyler Hemming
- Dylan Hughes
- Tyler Hughes
- Desmond Humphrey
- Lucio Ianiero
- Steve Jansen
- Jason Jordan
- Steve Kindel
- Tom Kouzmanis
- Josh Wagenaar
- Neil Wilkinson
- Chris Williams
- Murphy Wiredu
- Gregor Young
- Wojtek Zarzycki
- Peter Zezel

FIFA U-20 World Cup record

- 1977 – *Did not Qualify*
- 1979 – *Round 1*
- 1981 – *Did not Qualify*
- 1983 – *Did not Qualify*
- 1985 – *Round 1*
- 1987 – *Round 1*
- 1989 – *Did not Qualify*
- 1991 – *Did not Qualify*
- 1993 – *Did not Qualify*
- 1995 – *Did not Qualify*
- 1997 – *Round of 16*
- 1999 – *Did not Qualify*
- 2001 – *Round 1*
- 2003 – *Quarter-finals*
- 2005 – *Round 1*
- 2007 – *Round 1*
- 2009 – *Did not Qualify*

Honours

CONCACAF U-20 Championship

- **Winners (2)**: 1986, 1996

Football at the Jeux de la Francophonie

- **Winners (2)**: 1989, 1997

References

[1] (http://www.canadasoccer.com/tourney/FIFA_U20WC/national.asp?Press_ID=4601)
[2] (http://www.canadasoccer.com/news/viewArtical.asp?Press_ID=4367)
[3] (http://www.canadasoccer.com/news/viewArtical.asp?Press_ID=4239)

External links

- Canucks Abroad (http://www.canucks-abroad.com)
- Canadian Soccer Association (http://www.canadian-soccer.com)

USL First Division

Countries	United States Canada Puerto Rico
Confederation	CONCACAF
Founded	2005
Folded	2010
Conferences	1
Number of teams	3
Levels on pyramid	2
Promotion to	None
Relegation to	None
Domestic cup(s)	Lamar Hunt U.S. Open Cup Canadian Championship
International cup(s)	CFU Club Championship
Last champions	Puerto Rico Islanders (final champions) (2010)
Most championships	Seattle Sounders Vancouver Whitecaps (2 titles each)
TV partners	Fox Soccer Channel
Website	Official site in English [1]

The **United Soccer Leagues First Division** (usually referred to as simply **USL-1**) was a professional men's soccer league in the United States, Canada, and Puerto Rico.

Along with the North American Soccer League, it was one of the two leagues that formed the second tier of soccer in the United States and Canada league pyramid behind Major League Soccer. It was operated by the United Soccer Leagues (USL) and was the successor of the old **A-League**, which existed from 1997 until 2004, and was itself succeeded in 2011 by the USL Professional League.

History

- *See also A-League History*

When the A-League became the USL First Division in 2005, the league comprised 12 teams: Atlanta Silverbacks, Charleston Battery, Minnesota Thunder, Montreal Impact, Portland Timbers, Puerto Rico Islanders, Richmond Kickers, Rochester Raging Rhinos, Seattle Sounders, Toronto Lynx, Vancouver Whitecaps and Virginia Beach Mariners. The Calgary Mustangs, Edmonton Aviators and Syracuse Salty Dogs, all of whom competed in the final A-League season in 2004, folded during the offseason, and did not take up their places in the new league.

The Seattle Sounders won the inaugural USL1 championship, beating Richmond Kickers on penalty kicks in the championship game after a 1-1 tie in regulation time. The Vancouver Whitecaps won the first of their two USL1 titles in 2006 by beating the Rochester Raging Rhinos 3-0 in the championship game, while Seattle won their second title in 2007 by overcoming the Atlanta Silverbacks in a one-sided 4-0 final. Vancouver won their second USL1 championship in 2008 by beating the Puerto Rico Islanders 2-1 in the first USL1 final to feature no American teams; the championship went north of the border again in 2009 when Montreal Impact won their first USL1 title, beating Vancouver 6-3 on aggregate over two legs in the first all-Canadian affair.

On August 27, 2009, multi-national sports company Nike agreed to sell their stake in the United Soccer Leagues (USL) to Rob Hoskins and Alec Papadakis of Atlanta, Georgia-based **NuRock Soccer Holdings**, instead of to the USL Team Owner's Association (TOA), a group comprising the owners of several USL First Division clubs. In the months that followed, several prominent TOA members began to voice their concerns about the state of the league in general, its management structure and ownership model, the leadership of USL president Francisco Marcos, and about the sale of the league to NuRock, which the TOA felt was counter-productive and detrimental to the development of the league. Within several weeks, a number of TOA member clubs threatened to break away from USL and start their own league; this threat became official on November 10, 2009, when the majority of USL-1 clubs, as well as one of the expected 2010 expansion franchises, applied to the United States Soccer Federation, the Canadian Soccer Association, and FIFA for approval to create a new North American Soccer League,[1] reducing the league's membership to just three teams.

After lawsuits were filed and heated press statements exchanged, the United States Soccer Federation (USSF) declared they would sanction neither the NASL or the USL First Division in 2010, and ordered both "camps" to work together on a plan to temporarily allow their teams to play a 2010 season. The interim solution was announced on January 7, 2010 with the USSF running the new USSF D2 Pro League comprising clubs from both USL-1 and NASL.[2] All 12 teams from the USL First Division and the NASL competed in the USSF D2 Pro League in 2010, which was won by the Puerto Rico Islanders.

On September 8, 2010, the USL announced the formation of USL Pro which would merge the USL First Division and USL Second Division to begin play in 2011. The merger is meant to consolidate USL's position within the American professional soccer landscape and focus on commercial growth and professional development of soccer in 4 main regions throughout the U.S., Canada, and the Caribbean.[3] The First Division was formally dissolved following the completion of the temporary season to make way for USL Pro.[4]

Expansion and contraction

Prior to 2010, the league saw a steady rate of expansion and contraction. Richmond dropped down to the USL Second Division in 2006 to cut costs, Toronto dropped down to the USL Premier Development League in 2007 for similar reasons, and on March 30, 2007 the Virginia Beach Mariners folded just prior to the start of the 2007 season due to an ownership dispute which left the team without financing. These teams were replaced by two new teams: the Carolina RailHawks from the Triangle region of North Carolina, playing out of Cary, and California Victory, a team in Northern California under the ownership of Dmitry Piterman (chairman of Spanish team Deportivo Alavés) which folded after the end of the 2007 season, having played only one season.

In November 2008, the Atlanta Silverbacks announced that they would sit out the 2009 season to "reassess the landscape," and would possibly return at a future date.[5] Similarly, the Seattle Sounders left prior to the 2009 season due to the imminent entrance of Seattle Sounders FC into Major League Soccer. Their spot in the league was taken by the Cleveland City Stars, who won the USL Second Division title in 2008, and voluntarily moved up to USL-1 for the 2009 season,[6] only to fold at the end of the year. On December 2, 2009, Inside Minnesota Soccer reported that the USL had asked the City Stars to terminate the contracts of all the players, as the franchise was to be dissolved. Posting an email addressed to all players under contract with the Cleveland City Stars and written by team president Jonathan Ortlip and executive director Aaron Tredway, the club executives went on to accept the decision to terminate the franchise.[7]

On June 19, 2008, an announcement was made that an expansion slot had been awarded to a Tampa Bay, Florida-based franchise led by main investors Andrew Nestor (CEO) and Hinds Howard (Chairman) of Citrus Ventures.[8] The plan was for the club to join the league in 2010 and be named the Tampa Bay Rowdies.

Future expansion

Possible cities mentioned for future campaigns included Fort Lauderdale, Florida and Syracuse, New York. Syracuse had had a highly attended team in the A-League from 2002–2004, but it folded due to stadium issues, having ground-shared with the local baseball team. Fort Lauderdale also had a history of teams from the NASL, ASL, and USL First Division. There was also discussion that Argentinian team River Plate is interested in putting a second USL team in Puerto Rico, as well as discussion that recent start-up team, the San Diego Flash may also join either the USL or NASL.

Prior to the 2009 NASL split several other cities had been mentioned as being locations where future USL-1 franchises might be launched, including St. Louis, Missouri (led by the current PDL franchise St. Louis Lions),[9] Orlando, Florida (with Mexican side Pachuca being rumored as connected to it),[10] Milwaukee, Wisconsin, Detroit, Michigan, Hamilton, Ontario,[11] San Antonio, Texas[12] and Ottawa, Ontario. On September 1, 2009, a group from Ottawa formally applied for USL-1 team, contingent on the approval of updates to Lansdowne Park. The team would share a field with the Ottawa CFL team.[13] No further official announcements from the USL on any of these possibilities have been made.

Structure

Unlike most other nations, there is currently no system of merit-based promotion and relegation in the American and Canadian pyramids, meaning that the champions of USL-1 could not move up to Major League Soccer and, similarly, the worst teams in MLS were not in danger of being demoted to USL-1. However, some USL-1 teams had in the past chosen to take voluntary relegation to a lower level of the USL system, often to reduce operating costs, while teams had also decided to move up to USL-1 after finding success at the lower levels.

Playoff format

The top seven teams advanced to the playoff tournament, with the Commissioner's Cup winner (regular season champion) receiving a bye into the semi-finals. Each round consisted of two legs, the lower seeded team hosting the first leg, and the higher seed hosting the second. Prior to 2009, the final was played as a single leg at the higher seed's stadium. After the first legs were completed, the lowest remaining seed played the Commissioner's Cup winner, and the higher seeds played each other. The highest remaining seed hosted the penultimate game of the Finals. The playoffs started the week after the completion of the regular season, and typically ended in mid-October.

Teams

- Atlanta Silverbacks (2005–2008)
- Austin Aztex (2008–2010) **(2010 season played in USSF D2 Pro League)**
- California Victory (2007)
- Carolina RailHawks (2007–2009)
- Charleston Battery (2005–2009)
- Cleveland City Stars (2009)
- Miami FC (2006–2009)
- Minnesota Thunder (2005–2009)
- Montreal Impact (2005–2009)
- Portland Timbers (2005–2010) **(2010 season played in USSF D2 Pro League)**
- Richmond Kickers (2005)
- Rochester Rhinos (2005–2009)
- Seattle Sounders (2005–2008)
- Toronto Lynx (2005–2006)
- Vancouver Whitecaps (2005–2009)
- Virginia Beach Mariners (2005–2006)

- *See also A-League*

League champions / top goal scorer

Season	Winner	Score	Runner-up	Top Goalscorer(s)	Team	Goals
2009 USL D-1	**Montreal Impact**	6-3	Vancouver Whitecaps	Charles Gbeke	Vancouver Whitecaps	12
2008 USL D-1	**Vancouver Whitecaps**	2-1	Puerto Rico Islanders	Alex Afonso	Miami FC	15
2007 USL D-1	**Seattle Sounders**	4-0	Atlanta Silverbacks	Sébastien Le Toux and Charles Gbeke	Seattle Sounders and Montreal Impact	10
2006 USL D-1	**Vancouver Whitecaps**	3-0	Rochester Raging Rhinos	Romário and Cam Weaver	Miami FC and Seattle Sounders	18
2005 USL D-1	**Seattle Sounders**	1-1 (PK)	Richmond Kickers	Jason Jordan	Vancouver Whitecaps	17

Regular season champions (Commissioner's Cup Winners)

USL First Division

Season	Winner	Record (W-L-T)	Points	Playoff	Results (W-L-T)	Runners-Up	Record (W-L-T)	Points
2009 USL D-1	Portland Timbers	16-4-10	58	Lost in semifinal series	0-1-1	Carolina RailHawks FC	16-7-7	55
2008 USL D-1	Puerto Rico Islanders	15-6-9	54	Lost in final	1-2-0	Vancouver Whitecaps	15-7-8	53
2007 USL D-1	Seattle Sounders	16-6-6	54	Won Championship	4-1-0	Portland Timbers	14-5-9	51
2006 USL D-1	Montreal Impact	14-5-9	51	Lost in semifinal series	0-1-1	Rochester Raging Rhinos	13-4-11	50
2005 USL D-1	Montreal Impact	18-3-7	61	Lost in semifinal series	0-1-1	Rochester Raging Rhinos	15-7-6	51

Most Successful Clubs

Club	Championships	Runners-up	Regular Season Championships
Seattle Sounders	2	0	1
Vancouver Whitecaps	2	1	0
Montreal Impact	1	0	2
Puerto Rico Islanders	0	1	1
Portland Timbers	0	0	1
Atlanta Silverbacks	0	1	0
Richmond Kickers	0	1	0
Rochester Rhinos	0	1	0

League average attendance

Year	Regular season	Playoffs
2009	4,720	7,065
2008	5,164	7,786
2007	4,420	7,741
2006	4,667	5,998
2005	4,527	12,498

All-time USL leaders

All-Time Goal Leaders

Rank	Player	Goals
1	Mark Baena	86
2	Paul Conway	79
3	Doug Miller	77
4	Mauro Biello	76
5	**Jason Jordan**	70
6	**Eduardo Sebrango**	70
7	Chance Fry	68
8	Domenic Mobilio	65
9	Jamel Mitchell	64
10	**Kevin Jeffrey**	61

All-time appearances in the USL

Rank	Player	Appearances
1	Mauro Biello	320
2	Nick DeSantis	245
3	Lloyd Barker	242
4	**Nevio Pizzolito**	228
5	Scott Jenkins	220
6	Lenin Steenkamp	219
7	Bill Sedgewick	218
8	David Diplacido	217
9	**Steve Klein**	211

- Note: includes stats from the old A-League

See also
- Sports attendances

Notes
- (*) Puerto Rico can qualify for the CFU Club Championship via a domestic cup competition.

References
[1] "Teams Split From USL-1; To Form New League In 2010" (http://goal.com/en-us/news/66/united-states/2009/11/10/1616579/teams-split-from-usl-1-to-form-new-league-in-2010). Goal.com. 2009-11-10. . Retrieved 2009-11-20.
[2] "Division 2 Professional League To Operate in 2010" (http://www.ussoccer.com/News/Mens-National-Team/2010/01/Division-2-Professional-League-To-Operate-in-2010.aspx). ussoccer.com. 2010-01-07. . Retrieved 2010-01-09.
[3] "USL Restructures Professional Division" (http://usl1.uslsoccer.com/home/464019.html). www.uslsoccer.com. 2010-09-08. . Retrieved 2010-09-08.
[4] "USL Restructures Professional Division" (http://usl1.uslsoccer.com/home/464019.html). www.uslsoccer.com. 2010-09-08. . Retrieved 2010-09-10.

[5] http://www.atlantasilverbacks.com/news/displaynews.php?id=1046&cat=1
[6] http://www.canada.com/theprovince/news/sports/story.html?id=ec02001e-f74c-4ba1-9242-7a34cf0a3eaf
[7] http://www.insidemnsoccer.com/2009/12/02/cleveland-city-stars-release-players-from-contracts/
[8] Encina, Eduardo A. (2008-06-19). "Tampa Bay Rowdies to get new life in USL" (http://www.tampabay.com/sports/soccer/article633711.ece). St. Petersburg Times. . Retrieved 2008-06-20.
[9] http://www.stllions.com/
[10] "MLS: Atlanta Out! Orlando to USL. St Louis weak? Philly behind schedule..." (http://blogs.orlandosentinel.com/sports_soccerblog/2009/01/mls-atlanta-out.html). Orlando Sentinel. 2009-01-16. . Retrieved 2009-02-06.
[11] http://www.tsn.ca/soccer/story/?
[12] www.mysa.com date=4-18-09 id=268484&lid=headline&lpos=secStory_soccer
[13] http://www.uslsoccer.com/home/361425.html

External links

- Official site (http://usl1.uslsoccer.com/)
- Unofficial site created for the Fans, by the Fans (http://www.uslfans.com/)

@@

2005 United Soccer Leagues

The **2005 Season** was the 19th edition of the United Soccer Leagues season.

General

- A-League renamed USL First Division.
- Pro Soccer League renamed USL Second Division.
- The newly renamed top two divisions each become single table.
- The Syracuse Salty Dogs, Milwaukee Wave United, Edmonton Aviators, and Calgary Mustangs of the First Division folded following the 2004 season.
- The Utah Blitzz of the Second Division folded following the 2004 season.
- The Cincinnati Kings joined the Second Division, as an expansion club, for the 2005 season.
- The Westchester Flames, San Diego Gauchos, and California Gold switched from the Second Division to the PDL for the 2005 season.

Honors

Competition	Champion	Runner-Up	Regular Season Champion/Best USL team
USL First Division	Seattle Sounders	Richmond Kickers	Montreal Impact
USL Second Division	Charlotte Eagles	Western Mass Pioneers	Western Mass Pioneers
USL PDL	El Paso Patriots	Des Moines Menace	Orange County Blue Star
U.S. Open Cup	Los Angeles Galaxy (MLS)	FC Dallas (MLS)	Minnesota Thunder (Lost in Semi-final)

Premier Development League

- See 2005 PDL Season

Standings

First Division

Commissioner's Cup, bye to semifinal round of playoffs
    Bye to semifinal round of playoffs
    First round of playoffs

Pos	Club	Pts	Pld	W	L	T	GF	GA	GD	H2H Pts
1	Montreal Impact	61	28	18	3	7	37	15	+22	
2	Rochester Raging Rhinos	51	28	15	7	6	45	27	+18	
3	Vancouver Whitecaps	45	28	12	7	9	37	21	+16	
4	Seattle Sounders	44	28	11	6	11	33	25	+8	
5	Portland Timbers	39	28	10	9	9	40	42	−2	POR: 4 pts
6	Richmond Kickers	39	28	10	9	9	28	30	−2	RIC: 1 pt
7	Puerto Rico Islanders	38	28	10	10	8	46	43	+3	
8	Atlanta Silverbacks	33	28	10	15	3	40	52	−12	
9	Charleston Battery	32	28	9	14	5	27	36	−9	
10	Minnesota Thunder	31	28	7	11	10	37	42	−5	
11	Virginia Beach Mariners	28	28	7	14	7	26	39	−13	
12	Toronto Lynx	17	28	3	17	8	26	50	−24	

Playoffs

Each round except the final was a two-game aggregate goal series decided by extra time and a penalty shoot-out immediately following the second game of the series, if necessary. The away goals rule was not used as a tie-breaker. Tournament was re-seeded after the first round.

First Round					Semifinals					Final		
					1 Montreal Impact	2	1	3				
4 Seattle Sounders	1	2	3	4	Seattle Sounders	2	2	4				
5 Portland Timbers	0	0	0						4 Seattle Sounders (aet) (p)	1 (4)	
									6 Richmond Kickers	1 (3)	
					2 Rochester Raging Rhinos	1	1	2				
3 Vancouver Whitecaps	0	0	0 (4)	6	Richmond Kickers	3	1	4				
6 Richmond Kickers (aet) (p)	0	0	0 (5)									

See also

- United Soccer Leagues

External links

- Official USL Site [1]

2008 United Soccer Leagues

The **2008 Season** is the 22nd edition of the United Soccer Leagues season.

The season kicked off on Friday, April 12 with two First Division games, as the Charleston Battery visited Miami FC and the Montreal Impact visited the Vancouver Whitecaps.

General

- Changes in the First Division: the California Victory take the 2008 season off, leaving 11 teams playing a 30-game schedule.
- Changes in the Second Division: the Pittsburgh Riverhounds return from hiatus, and Real Maryland FC join as an expansion team. However, the Cincinnati Kings and New Hampshire Phantoms drop to the PDL. 10 teams play a 20-game schedule this season.
- In the PDL, 5 teams withdrew for the 2008 season, while 7 expansion teams and the two voluntary relegations increase the league to 67 teams in 10 divisions across 4 conferences. Teams play a 16-game league schedule.

Honors

Competition	Champion	Runner-Up	Regular Season Champion/Best USL team
USL First Division	Vancouver Whitecaps	Puerto Rico Islanders	Puerto Rico Islanders
USL Second Division	Cleveland City Stars	Charlotte Eagles	Charlotte Eagles
USL PDL	Thunder Bay Chill	Laredo Heat	Michigan Bucks
U.S. Open Cup	D.C. United (MLS)	Charleston Battery (USL-1)	Charleston Battery

Standings

First Division

Commissioner's Cup, bye to semifinal round of playoffs
    First round of playoffs

Pos	Club	Pts	Pld	W	L	T	GF	GA	GD	H2H Pts
1	Puerto Rico Islanders	54	30	15	6	9	43	23	+20	
2	Vancouver Whitecaps	53	30	15	7	8	34	28	+6	
3	Montreal Impact	42	30	12	12	6	33	28	+5	
4	Rochester Rhinos	41[†]	30	11	10	9	35	32	+3	
5	Charleston Battery	40	30	11	12	7	34	36	−2	CHA: 4 pts
6	Seattle Sounders	40	30	10	10	10	37	36	+1	SEA: 4 pts
7	Minnesota Thunder	39	30	10	11	9	40	38	+2	
8	Carolina RailHawks	37	30	9	11	10	34	43	−9	
9	Miami FC	34	30	8	12	10	28	34	−6	MIA: 7 pts
10	Atlanta Silverbacks	34	30	8	12	10	37	50	−13	ATL: 1 pt
11	Portland Timbers	31	30	7	13	10	26	33	−7	

Tie-breaker order: 1. Head-to-head points; 2. Total wins; 3. Goal difference; 4. Goals for; 5. Lottery

[†] Rochester deducted 1 point for use of an ineligible player on August 10, 2008[1]

Playoffs

Teams will be re-seeded for semifinal matchups

```
First Round              Semifinals              Final
September 26/28          October 3/5             October 12

1 Puerto Rico Islanders
  bye
                         Puerto Rico Islanders  0    3  3
                       1 (AET)
                         Rochester Rhinos       2    0  2
4 Rochester Rhinos   2 0 2  4
5 Charleston Battery 0 1 1
                                                              Puerto Rico Islanders  1
                                                            1
                                                              Vancouver Whitecaps    2
                                                            2
3 Montreal Impact    1 3 4
6 Seattle Sounders   2 1 3
                                       2         Vancouver Whitecaps  0  2  2
                         Montreal Impact        1    0  1
2 Vancouver Whitecaps 2 3 5  3
7 Minnesota Thunder  0 4 4
```

Awards and All-League team

First Team

F: Alex Afonso (Miami FC); Macoumba Kandji (Atlanta Silverbacks)

M: Osvaldo Alonso (Charleston Battery); Stephen deRoux (Minnesota Thunder); Martin Nash (Vancouver Whitecaps); Jonathan Steele (Puerto Rico Islanders) (league MVP)

D: Cristian Arrieta (Puerto Rico Islanders) (Defender of the Year); Taylor Graham (Seattle Sounders); David Hayes (Atlanta Silverbacks); Nevio Pizzolitto (Montreal Impact)

G: Bill Gaudette (Puerto Rico Islanders) (Goalkeeper of the Year)

Coach: Colin Clarke (Puerto Rico Islanders) (Coach of the Year)

Second Team

F: Sebastien Le Toux (Seattle Sounders); Eduardo Sebrango (Vancouver Whitecaps)

M: Leonardo Di Lorenzo (Montreal Impact); Johnny Menyongar (Rochester Rhinos); Ricardo Sanchez (Minnesota Thunder); Matt Watson (Carolina RailHawks)

D: Wesley Charles and Takashi Hirano (Vancouver Whitecaps); Cameron Knowles (Portland Timbers); Scott Palguta (Rochester Rhinos)

G: Matt Jordan (Montreal Impact)

Second Division

Place	Team	P	W	L	T	GF	GA	GD	Points
1	Charlotte Eagles	20	13	2	5	45	15	+30	44
2	Richmond Kickers	20	14	4	2	48	20	+28	44
3	Cleveland City Stars	20	10	3	7	33	16	+17	37
4	Crystal Palace Baltimore	20	11	8	1	30	30	0	34
5	Harrisburg City Islanders	20	7	3	10	33	20	+13	31
6	Western Mass Pioneers	20	5	9	6	19	29	-10	20†
7	Wilmington Hammerheads	20	4	9	7	32	33	-1	19
8	Pittsburgh Riverhounds	20	4	10	6	25	37	-12	18
9	Bermuda Hogges	20	5	13	2	21	50	-29	17
10	Real Maryland Monarchs	20	3	15	2	15	51	-36	10†

† *Western Mass and Real Maryland deducted 1 point*

Playoffs

Playoff Bracket

	First Round August 13			Semifinals August 16			Final August 23	
			1	**Charlotte Eagles**	2			
4	**Crystal Palace Baltimore** (AET/PK)	2 (7)	4	Crystal Palace Baltimore	1			
5	Harrisburg City Islanders	2 (6)				1	Charlotte Eagles	1
						3	**Cleveland City Stars**	2
			2	Richmond Kickers	0			
3	**Cleveland City Stars**	4	3	**Cleveland City Stars** (AET)	1			
6	Western Mass Pioneers	2						

Awards and All-League team

First Team

F: Jorge Herrera (Charlotte Eagles); Boyzzz Khumalo (Pittsburgh Riverhounds); Dustin Swinehart (Charlotte Eagles) (league MVP)

M: Mike Burke (Richmond Kickers); Floyd Franks (Cleveland City Stars); Shintaro Harada (Crystal Palace Baltimore)

D: Brady Bryant and Steve Shak (Charlotte Eagles); Sascha Gorres (Richmond Kickers); Mark Schulte (Cleveland City Stars) (Defender of the Year)

G: Terry Boss (Charlotte Eagles)

Coach: Mark Steffens (Charlotte Eagles) (Coach of the Year)

Rookie of the Year: Stanley Nyazamba (Richmond Kickers)

Second Team

F: Gary Brooks (Crystal Palace Baltimore); Sallieu Bundu (Cleveland City Stars); Jeff Deren (Western Mass Pioneers)

M: Trey Alexander (Wilmington Hammerheads); Justin Evans (Pittsburgh Riverhounds); Matthew Mbuta (Crystal Palace Baltimore)

D: Dustin Bixler (Harrisburg City Islanders); Trevor McEachron (Richmond Kickers); Federico Molinari (Western Mass Pioneers); Dame Walters (Wilmington Hammerheads)

G: Ronnie Pascale (Richmond Kickers)

Premier Development League

- See 2008 PDL Season

References

[1] "Rhinos penalized for infraction" (http://usl1.uslsoccer.com/recentnews/269957.html). United Soccer Leagues. August 15, 2008. . Retrieved June 28, 2011.

External links

- Official USL Site (http://www.uslsoccer.com)

2009 United Soccer Leagues

The **2009 season** is the 23rd season played by the United Soccer Leagues. Season titles will be contested by 20 professional men's clubs in the USL First Division and USL Second Division, as well as 37 professional and amateur women's clubs in the W-League and 68 professional and amateur men's teams in the USL Premier Development League.

The First Division season kicked off on April 11 with the US Open Cup finalist Charleston Battery and host defending champions Vancouver Whitecaps FC playing to a scoreless tie, while the Carolina RailHawks defeating the visiting Minnesota Thunder 2-1. The season ended on September 20 with the Charleston Battery defeating hosts Minnesota Thunder 3-2. As a change for this season, the Finals will follow the rest of the playoffs in being two legs.[1] The playoffs started on September 24, and ended on October 17 with the Montreal Impact defeating Vancouver Whitecaps FC on a 6-3 aggregate score.

The Second Division season started on April 17 with the Pittsburgh Riverhounds and host Crystal Palace Baltimore playing to a scoreless tie. The regular season ended on August 15 with three games. The Richmond Kickers captured the title in the playoffs with a 3-1 win over the Charlotte Eagles on August 29.

Portland

Vancouver

Montreal

Rochester

Austin

Carolina

Charleston

Miami

Cleveland

Minnesota

Harrisburg

Wilmington

Baltimore

Maryland

Richmond

Pittsburgh

Charlotte

Western Mass.

2009 USL-1 (red) and USL-2 (green) franchises. Not shown: Puerto Rico Islanders, Bermuda Hogges.

General

- Changes in the First Division: the Cleveland City Stars were promoted from Second Division and the Austin Aztex were added as an expansion team. The Atlanta Silverbacks went on hiatus for the season, and the Seattle Sounders were replaced by an expansion MLS team.
- Changes in the Second Division: the Cleveland City Stars were promoted to the First Division.
- In the PDL, 9 teams withdrew for the 2009 season, while 10 expansion teams increase the league to 68 teams in 8 divisions across 4 conferences. Teams play a 16-game league schedule.
- In the W-League, 6 teams withdrew for the 2009 season, while 2 expansion teams were added, leaving the league at 37 members. Sky Blue and Washington Freedom were given WPS teams, with Washington playing their reserves in the W-League and Sky Blue selling their W-League team.

Honors

Competition	Champion	Runner-Up	Regular Season Champion/Best USL team
USL First Division	Montreal Impact	Vancouver Whitecaps FC	Portland Timbers
USL Second Division	Richmond Kickers	Charlotte Eagles	Wilmington Hammerheads
USL PDL	Ventura County Fusion	Chicago Fire Premier	Reading Rage
U.S. Open Cup	Seattle Sounders FC	D.C. United	Rochester Rhinos
USL W-League	Pali Blues	Washington Freedom Reserves	Hudson Valley Quickstrike Lady Blues

First Division

Season	2009
Goals scored	388
Average goals/game	2.35
Biggest home win	9 – 0 (Carolina vs Miami)
Biggest away win	4 – 1 (Portland @ Rochester) 3 – 0 (Portland @ Miami, Carolina @ Cleveland, Rochester @ Cleveland)
Highest scoring	9 – 0 (Carolina vs Miami)
Longest winning run	5 (Portland, Puerto Rico)
Longest unbeaten run	24 (Portland)
Longest losing run	6 (Miami)
Highest attendance	14,103 (Portland)
Lowest attendance	67 (Miami)
Average attendance	4,702
← 2008 2010 →	

Regular season

Standings

Commissioner's Cup, bye to semifinal round of playoffs
    Quarterfinal round of playoffs

Pos	Club	Pts	Pld	W	L	T	GF	GA	GD	H2H Pts
1	Portland Timbers	58	30	16	4	10	45	19	+26	
2	Carolina RailHawks	55	30	16	7	7	43	19	+24	
3	Puerto Rico Islanders	53	30	15	7	8	44	31	+13	PUE: 6 pts
4	Charleston Battery	53	30	14	6	10	33	21	+12	CHA: 3 pts
5	Montreal Impact	44	30	12	10	8	32	31	+1	
6	Rochester Rhinos	43	30	11	9	10	34	32	+2	
7	Vancouver Whitecaps	42	30	11	10	9	42	36	+6	
8	Minnesota Thunder	31	30	7	13	10	39	44	−5	
9	Miami FC	29	30	8	17	5	26	52	−26	
10	Austin Aztex	21[†]	30	5	17	8	28	51	−23	
11	Cleveland City Stars	19	30	4	19	7	22	52	−30	

[†] Austin deducted two points for fielding an ineligible player on July 25, 2009[2]

Results

Abbreviation and Color Key:
Austin Aztex - AUS · Carolina RailHawks - CAR · Charleston Battery - CHA · Cleveland City Stars - CLE · Miami FC - MIA · Minnesota Thunder - MIN · Montreal Impact - MTL · Portland Timbers - POR · Puerto Rico Islanders - PUE · Rochester Rhinos - ROC · Vancouver Whitecaps FC - VAN

Win · Loss · Tie · Home

Playoffs

Teams will be re-seeded for semifinal matchups

	Quarterfinals					Semifinals					Final			
2	Carolina RailHawks FC	0	0	**0**										
7	**Vancouver Whitecaps FC**	1	0	**1**										
					1	Portland Timbers	1	3	**4**					
					7	**Vancouver Whitecaps FC**	2	3	**5**					
										5	Montreal Impact	3	3	**6**
3	**Puerto Rico Islanders**	1	4	**5**						7	Vancouver Whitecaps FC	2	1	**3**
6	Rochester Rhinos	2	1	**3**										
					3	Puerto Rico Islanders	1	1	**2**					
					5	**Montreal Impact**	2	2	**4**					
4	Charleston Battery	0	1	**1**										
5	**Montreal Impact**	2	2	**4**										

Quarterfinals

September 24, 2009 7:05 PM EDT	**Puerto Rico Islanders**	1 – 2	**Rochester Rhinos**	Marina Auto Stadium Rochester, New York Referee: Chris Penso (United States)
	Arrieta 7' Hansen 68' Addlery 72'	(Report) [3]	Bertz 64' Ball 71' Short 74'	

September 24, 2009 7:45 PM EDT	**Charleston Battery**	0 – 2	**Montreal Impact**	Saputo Stadium Montreal, Quebec Attendance: 11,282 Referee: Dave Gantar (Canada)
	Bobo 10', 45'	(Report) [4]	Testo 10' Di Lorenzo 12' Placentino 88' 88'	

September 24, 2009 7:30 PM PDT	**Carolina RailHawks FC** Low 78' Paladini 80'	**0 – 1** (Report) [5]	**Vancouver Whitecaps FC** Versailles 64' Edwini-Bonsu 77'	Swangard Stadium Burnaby, British Columbia Attendance: 5,135 Referee: Fabrizio Romano (Canada)
September 27, 2009 5:00 PM EDT	**Vancouver Whitecaps FC** Bellisomo 43' Nash 59' Martin 75'	**0 – 0** (Report) [6]	**Carolina RailHawks FC** Rusin 52' Plotkin 76'	WakeMed Soccer Park Cary, North Carolina Attendance: 2,471 Referee: Niko Bratsis (United States)
September 27, 2009 7:00 PM ADT	**Rochester Rhinos** Sancho 24', 29' Nunes 82'	**1 – 4** (Report) [7]	**Puerto Rico Islanders** Noël 12', 80' Addlery 40', 90' 84'	Juan Ramón Loubriel Stadium Bayamón, Puerto Rico Attendance: 4,232 Referee: Jose Rivero (United States)
September 27, 2009 7:00 PM EDT	**Montreal Impact** deRoux 16' Pizzolitto 23' Donatelli 74' 82'	**2 – 1** (Report) [8]	**Charleston Battery** Fuller 16' 72' Wilson 76'	Blackbaud Stadium Charleston, South Carolina Attendance: 2,311 Referee: Mark Kadlecik (United States)

Semifinals

October 1, 2009 7:30 PM EDT	**Puerto Rico Islanders** Jones 6' Steele 31'	**1 – 2** (Report) [9]	**Montreal Impact** Donatelli 8' Brown 20' Pizzolitto 58'	Saputo Stadium Montreal, Quebec Attendance: 9,835 Referee: Carol Anne Chenard (CAN)
October 1, 2009 7:30 PM PDT	**Portland Timbers** Pore 44'	**1 – 2** (Report) [10]	**Vancouver Whitecaps FC** Gbeke 25' Reda 45' Haber 49' James 66' Versailles 76'	Swangard Stadium Burnaby, British Columbia Attendance: 4,516 Referee: Geoff Gamble (CAN)
October 4, 2009 7:00 PM ADT	**Montreal Impact** Byers 2' deRoux 16' Pizzolitto 24' Joqueviel 81' Sebrango 90'	**2 – 1** (Report) [11]	**Puerto Rico Islanders** Vélez 44' Hansen 86' (pen.) Nuñez 90'	Juan Ramón Loubriel Stadium Bayamón, Puerto Rico Attendance: 5,101 Referee: Oscar Ortiz (USA)

October 4, 2009 4:00 PM PDT	Vancouver Whitecaps FC Haber ⚽ 4', 62' Nash ⚽ 60' James ⚽ 71'	3–3	(Report) [12]	Portland Timbers Farber ⚽ 10', 43' McManus 26' Pore 66' Nimo ⚽ 83' López 90'	PGE Park Portland, Oregon Attendance: 14,283 Referee: Gilario Grajeda (USA)

Finals

October 10, 2009 6:30 PM PDT	Montreal Impact Pejic ⚽ 45' (Own goal) Byers ⚽ 63' Sebrango ⚽ 89'	3–2	(Report) [13]	Vancouver Whitecaps FC Nash 51' Haber ⚽ 56' James ⚽ 65', 66'	Swangard Stadium Burnaby, British Columbia Attendance: 5,886 Referee: Carol Anne Chenard (CAN)

October 17, 2009 2:30 PM EDT	Vancouver Whitecaps FC Bellsomo 21' Pejic 29' Moose 56' Toure ⚽ 44'	1–3	(Report) [14]	Montreal Impact Donatelli ⚽ 30' (pen.) Gjertsen ⚽ 40' Brown ⚽ 42'	Saputo Stadium Montreal, Quebec Attendance: 13,034 Referee: Dave Gantar

Awards and All-League team

F: Charles Gbeke (VAN), Keita Mandjou (POR), Johnny Menyongar (ROC)
M: Daniel Paladini (CAR), Ryan Pore (POR), Ricardo Sánchez (MIN)
D: Nelson Akwari (CHA), Cristian Arrieta, (PR), Matt Bobo (CHA), David Hayes, (POR)
G: Steve Cronin (POR) (**Goalkeeper of the Year**)
Coach:

Second Division

Season	2009
Champions	Wilmington Hammerheads (Regular Season); Richmond Kickers (playoffs)
Goals scored	252
Average goals/game	2.80
Biggest home win	6–0 (Charlotte vs. Bermuda)
Biggest away win	6–3 (Wilmington @ Charlotte) 3–0 (Charlotte @ Real Maryland)
Highest scoring	7–2 (Richmond vs Bermuda) 6–3 (Wilmington @ Charlotte)
Longest winning run	5 (Wilmington)
Longest unbeaten run	6 (Richmond)
Longest losing run	5 (Bermuda)
Highest attendance	4,010 (Richmond)
Lowest attendance	200 (Bermuda)

Average attendance	1,686

← 2008
2010 →

Regular season

Standings

Pos	Team	Pld	W	L	T	GF	GA	GD	Pts
1	Wilmington Hammerheads	20	12	3	5	42	24	+18	41
2	Richmond Kickers	20	11	3	6	39	18	+21	39
3	Harrisburg City Islanders	20	9	7	4	31	23	+8	31
4	Charlotte Eagles	20	8	5	7	40	28	+12	31
5	Real Maryland Monarchs	20	8	10	2	22	31	−9	26
6	Crystal Palace Baltimore	20	6	9	5	16	20	−4	23
7	Western Mass Pioneers	20	6	9	5	21	34	−13	23
8	Pittsburgh Riverhounds	20	6	10	4	18	27	−9	22
9	Bermuda Hogges	20	4	12	4	19	43	−24	16

Purple indicates league title clinched
Green indicates playoff berth clinched

Results

Abbreviation and Color Key:
Bermuda Hogges - BMU • Charlotte Eagles - CHA • Crystal Palace Baltimore - CPB
Harrisburg City Islanders - HAR • Pittsburgh Riverhounds - PIT • Real Maryland Monarchs - RMM
Richmond Kickers - RIC • Western Mass Pioneers - WMA • Wilmington Hammerheads - WIL
Win • Loss • Tie • Home

Club	Match																			
	1	2	3	4	5	6	7	8	9	10	11	12	13	14	15	16	17	18	19	20
Bermuda Hogges	CPB	RMM	HAR	RIC	WIL	WIL	RMY	WIL	CHA	PIT	HAR	CPB	WMA	PIT	PIT	RIC	WMA	WMA	CHA	RMY
	2-0	3-2	2-1	1-0	0-0	0-1	1-0	1-0	6-0	1-0	3-0	1-2	2-2	1-2	1-0	7-2	5-0	2-2	1-1	4-3
Charlotte Eagles	WIL	CPB	WIL	RIC	CPB	HAR	PIT	BMU	WMA	RIC	HAR	WIL	RIC	WMA	RMM	RMM	CPB	BMU	PIT	WMA
	2-2	0-2	3-6	1-1	1-2	3-0	5-1	6-0	2-0	2-2	0-0	2-3	3-0	5-0	1-1	0-3	0-0	1-1	1-3	3-0
Crystal Palace Baltimore	PIT	BMU	CHA	WIL	RMM	WMA	CHA	RIC	WMA	RMM	WMA	WIL	BMU	RMM	HAR	HAR	RIC	CHA	HAR	PIT
	0-0	2-0	0-2	3-0	2-0	1-0	1-2	1-1	0-0	0-1	2-1	2-1	1-2	0-1	3-1	2-0	1-2	0-0	0-0	1-0
Harrisburg City Islanders	RIC	WMA	BMU	PIT	PIT	CHA	RMM	RIC	BMU	RMM	CHA	WIL	CPB	CPB	PIT	WIL	RIC	RMM	CPB	WMA
	2-2	3-1	2-1	3-0	0-1	3-0	2-3	5-0	3-0	4-0	0-0	3-2	3-1	2-0	1-0	1-2	0-1	0-0	0-0	2-1
Pittsburgh Riverhounds	CPB	RIC	RMM	HAR	HAR	CHA	WIL	BMU	RIC	WMA	RIC	BMU	BMU	RMM	HAR	WMA	WMA	WIL	CHA	CPB
	0-0	1-1	2-1	3-0	0-1	5-1	1-3	1-0	0-2	0-0	1-2	1-2	1-0	2-1	1-0	1-1	3-0	0-2	1-3	1-0

Real Maryland Monarchs	BMU	PIT	CPB	WMA	BMU	CPB	HAR	WMA	RIC	HAR	WIL	CPB	PIT	WIL	CHA	CHA	RIC	HAR	BMU	WIL
	3-2	2-1	2-0	3-0	1-0	0-1	2-3	2-0	1-0	4-0	3-0	0-1	2-1	3-1	1-1	0-3	1-0	0-0	4-3	2-0
Richmond Kickers	HAR	RIC	WMA	BMU	CHA	CPB	WMA	HAR	RMM	PIT	CHA	PIT	CHA	BMU	CPB	WIL	HAR	RMM	WIL	WIL
	2-2	1-1	0-2	1-0	1-1	1-1	2-0	5-0	1-0	0-2	2-2	1-2	3-0	7-2	1-2	3-2	0-1	1-0	0-1	2-2
Western Mass Pioneers	HAR	RIC	CPB	RMM	WIL	CPB	RIC	CPB	RMM	CHA	PIT	BMU	WIL	CHA	BMU	BMU	PIT	PIT	HAR	CHA
	3-1	0-2	1-0	3-0	2-1	0-0	2-0	2-1	2-0	2-0	0-0	2-2	4-0	5-0	5-0	2-2	1-1	3-0	2-1	3-0
Wilmington Hammerheads	CHA	CPB	CHA	BMU	BMU	WMA	PIT	BMU	CPB	RMM	HAR	CHA	WMA	RMM	RIC	HAR	PIT	RIC	RMM	RIC
	2-2	3-0	3-6	0-0	0-1	2-1	1-3	1-0	2-1	0-3	3-2	2-3	4-0	3-1	3-2	1-2	0-2	0-1	2-0	2-2

Playoffs

	Quarterfinals			Semifinals			Final	
			1	Wilmington Hammerheads	0			
4	**Charlotte Eagles**	3	4	**Charlotte Eagles**	1			
5	Real Maryland Monarchs	1				2	**Richmond Kickers**	3
						4	Charlotte Eagles	1
			2	**Richmond Kickers** (AET)	1			
			3	Harrisburg City Islanders	0			

First Round

August 19, 2009   **Real Maryland Monarchs**   1 – 3   **Charlotte Eagles**   Restart Field

Brooks ⚽ 83', 54', 90+'   Report [15]   Herrera ⚽ 4' (pen.)
Lewis 68'   Swinehart ⚽ 16'
King 89'   Bentos ⚽ 90' 90+'
Funicello 90'

Charlotte, North Carolina
Attendance: 760
Referee: Mark Kadlecik (United States)

Semifinals

August 22, 2009   7:00 PM EDT   **Harrisburg City Islanders**   0 – 1 (AET)   **Richmond Kickers**   University of Richmond Stadium, Richmond, Virginia

Baker 43'   (Report) [16]   Worthen 33'
Velten 63'   Hunter 117'
                             Delicâte ⚽ 120'

Attendance: 1,923
Referee: Mike Andrews (United States)

August 22, 2009   7:00 PM EDT   **Charlotte Eagles**   1 – 0   **Wilmington Hammerheads**   Legion Stadium, Wilmington, North Carolina

Williams 61'   (Report) [17]   Watson 36'
Herrera 62'
Swinehart 80'
Bentos ⚽ 85'

Attendance: 2,783
Referee: Dan Fitzgerald (United States)

Final

August 29, 2009 8:00 PM EDT	**Charlotte Eagles** Martins ⚽ 14' Nunes 41' Williams 46' Ceus 85'	1 – 3 (Report) [18]	**Richmond Kickers** Elcock ⚽ 63' DiRaimondo ⚽ 83' Bulow ⚽ 86' (pen.)	University of Richmond Stadium, Richmond, Virginia Attendance: 2,991 Referee: Tony Russo (United States)

Awards and All-League team

First Team
F: Matthew Delicâte (Richmond Kickers), Jamie Watson (WIL) (**MVP**)
M: Ty Shipalane (HAR), Kenny Bundy (WIL), Mike Burke (RIC), Jorge Herrera (CHA)
D: Dustin Bixler (HAR), John Borrajo (RMD), Shintaro Harada (CPB), Yomby William (RIC) (**Defender of the Year**)
G: Ronnie Pascale (RIC) (**Goalkeeper of the Year**)
Coach: David Irving (WIL)
Rookie of the Year: Ty Shipalane, HAR

Second Team
F: Almir Barbosa (WMA), Damico Coddington (BER), Chad Severs (HAR)
M: Justin Evans (PIT), Jamie Franks (WIL), Amaury Nunes (CHA), Val Teixeira (CPB)
D: Colin Falvey (WIL), Sascha Gorres (RIC), Andrew Marshall (CPB)
G: Chase Harrison (HAR)

References

[1] "2009 USL-1 season details unveiled" (http://www.uslsoccer.com/USL1news/301755.html). www.uslsoccer.com. January 23, 2009. . Retrieved 2009-01-30.
[2] "Austin receives two point deduction" (http://usl1.uslsoccer.com/home/351805.html). www.uslsoccer.com. July 29, 2009. . Retrieved 2009-08-11.

External links

- Official USL Site (http://www.uslsoccer.com)

Pan American Games

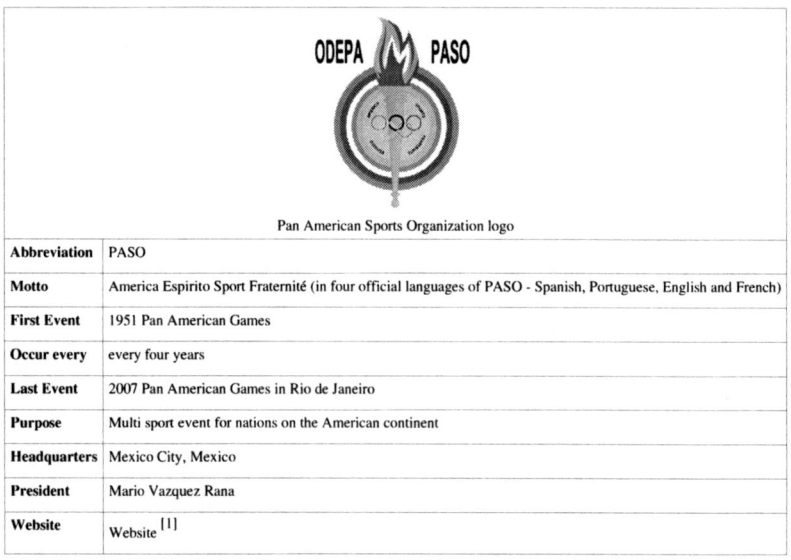

Pan American Sports Organization logo

Abbreviation	PASO
Motto	America Espirito Sport Fraternité (in four official languages of PASO - Spanish, Portuguese, English and French)
First Event	1951 Pan American Games
Occur every	every four years
Last Event	2007 Pan American Games in Rio de Janeiro
Purpose	Multi sport event for nations on the American continent
Headquarters	Mexico City, Mexico
President	Mario Vazquez Rana
Website	Website [1]

The **Pan American Games** (**Pan Am Games**) is a multi-sport event between competitors from all nations in Americas, held every four years in the year before the summer Olympic Games. The games were last held in Rio de Janeiro, Brazil in 2007. The next will be in Guadalajara, Mexico in 2011, followed by the 2015 games in Toronto, Canada.

History

The idea of holding a Pan American Games grew from the Central American Games which were first organized in the 1920s. In 1932, a first proposal was made for Pan American Games, and the Pan American Sports Organization (Organización Deportiva Panamericana; ODEPA/PASO) was established. The first games were scheduled to be staged in Buenos Aires in 1943, but World War II caused them to be postponed until 1951. Since then, the Games have been held every four years, with participation at the most recent event at over 5,000 athletes from 42 countries.[1]

However, for certain sports on the program, such as swimming, the Pan American Games have lost status in the United States, and have not received much attention in the sporting press. The Americans had sent their "B" swimming team to Winnipeg in 1999, in contrast to the 1967 edition where they fielded many rising stars such as Mark Spitz. No major USA television network has covered the last 3 editions of the Games, while newspapers sent second-string reporters and the stories never made front page news. Many high profile athletes, of all nationalities, such as US champion sprinters and Brazilian football players, were in Europe during these Pan Ams, taking part in professional events. South American nations (with the exception of Uruguay) did not send their under-23 male soccer teams after the organizing committee refused to pay appearance money to CONMEBOL. In Canada, there was plenty of coverage, including a nightly two-hour program on CBC, with an additional hour on local affiliate CBWT, French-language coverage on Radio-Canada, plus daytime coverage on TSN. By 2003, the Pan American Games were once again neglected by the media. Generally, the Pan American Games receive plenty of attention in most Latin American countries. The 2007 edition, held in Rio de Janeiro, Brazil, has prompted the Organizing

Committee to restore important venues such as the Estádio do Maracanã and build a new Olympic Village. In the United States, the Rio Games were broadcast live and on a delayed basis by ESPN Deportes, ESPN's Spanish-language sports network.[1]

Winter Games

There have been attempts to hold **Pan American Winter Games** as well, but these have been without much success. An initial attempt to hold winter events was made by the organizers of the 1951 Pan American Games in Buenos Aires, who planned to stage winter events later in the year but dropped the idea for lack of interest.[1]

Lake Placid, New York, tried to organize Winter Games in 1959, but again not enough countries expressed interest and the plans were canceled.[1]

In 1988, members of PASO voted to hold the first Pan American Winter Games at Las Leñas, Argentina in September 1989. It was further agreed that Winter Games would be held every four years. Lack of snow forced postponement of the games until September 16–22, 1990, when eight countries sent 97 athletes to Las Lenas. Of that total, 76 were from just three countries: Argentina, Canada, and the United States. Weather was unseasonably warm and again there was little snow, so only three Alpine Skiing events—the Slalom, Giant Slalom, and Super G—were staged. The U.S. and Canada combined to win all 18 medals.[1]

PASO awarded the second Pan American Winter Games to Santiago, Chile for 1993. The United States warned that it would not take part unless a full schedule of events was held. The Santiago organizing committee eventually gave up and the idea has not been revived since.[1]

Editions

Summer

Map of Pan American Games locations (host cities in red dots). Countries that have hosted one Pan Am Games are shaded green, while countries that have hosted two or more are shaded blue.

Games	Year	Host
I	1951	Buenos Aires, Argentina
II	1955	Mexico City, Mexico
III	1959	Chicago, United States
IV	1963	São Paulo, Brazil
V	1967	Winnipeg, Canada
VI	1971	Cali, Colombia
VII	1975	Mexico City, Mexico
VIII	1979	San Juan, Puerto Rico
IX	1983	Caracas, Venezuela
X	1987	Indianapolis, United States
XI	1991	Havana, Cuba
XII	1995	Mar del Plata, Argentina
XIII	1999	Winnipeg, Canada
XIV	2003	Santo Domingo, Dominican Republic
XV	2007	Rio de Janeiro, Brazil
XVI	2011	*Guadalajara, Mexico*
XVII	2015	*Toronto, Canada*

Winter

Games	Year	Host
I	1990	Las Leñas, Argentina

Medals table

The table below gives an overview of the all-time medal count of the Pan American Games. As of the 2007 Pan American Games, Aruba, the British Virgin Islands and Saint Kitts and Nevis have yet to win a medal.[2] [3]

Rank	Nation	Gold	Silver	Bronze	Total
1	United States	1769	1300	867	3936
2	Cuba	781	531	484	1796
3	Canada	347	546	684	1577
4	Argentina	258	286	372	916
5	Brazil	239	284	402	925
6	Mexico	155	217	410	782
7	Venezuela	73	156	224	453
8	Colombia	58	109	160	327
9	Chile	36	69	109	214
10	Puerto Rico	21	71	113	205

11		Jamaica	21	37	57	115
12		Dominican Republic	19	43	88	150
13		Ecuador	14	13	37	64
14		Uruguay	11	21	41	73
15		Trinidad and Tobago	8	18	25	51
16		Guatemala	7	11	32	50
17		Bahamas	6	12	10	28
18		Peru	5	28	54	87
19		Netherlands Antilles	4	9	16	29
20		Costa Rica	4	6	8	18
21		Panama	3	23	30	56
22		Suriname	3	2	5	10
23		Guyana	2	4	11	17
24		El Salvador	1	6	12	19
25		Bermuda	1	4	3	8
26		Antigua and Barbuda	1	0	3	4
27		Nicaragua	0	4	7	11
28		United States Virgin Islands	0	4	6	10
29		Barbados	0	3	7	10
30		Cayman Islands	0	3	0	3
31		Haiti	0	2	5	7
32		Honduras	0	1	4	5
32		Paraguay	0	1	4	5
34		Bolivia	0	1	2	3
34		Grenada	0	1	2	3
36		Dominica	0	1	1	2
37		Belize	0	0	2	2
37		Saint Lucia	0	0	2	2
39		Saint Vincent and the Grenadines	0	0	1	1
		Total	3845	3827	4300	111972

Participating Nations

- Antigua and Barbuda
- Argentina
- Aruba
- Bahamas
- Barbados
- Belize
- Bermuda
- Bolivia
- Brazil
- British Virgin Islands
- Canada
- Cayman Islands
- Chile
- Colombia
- Costa Rica
- Cuba
- Dominica
- Dominican Republic
- Ecuador
- El Salvador
- Grenada
- Guatemala
- Guyana
- Haiti
- Honduras
- Jamaica
- Mexico
- Netherlands Antilles
- Nicaragua
- Panama
- Paraguay
- Peru
- Puerto Rico
- Saint Kitts and Nevis
- Saint Lucia
- Saint Vincent and the Grenadines
- Suriname
- Trinidad and Tobago
- United States
- Uruguay
- Venezuela
- U.S. Virgin Islands

Sports

According to Pan American Sports Organization rules all 28 current Olympic sports, plus optional sports that is popular throughout the Americas can be played at a single games.[4]

Pan American Torch

Since the first Pan American Games, a torch is lit in the same way as the Olympic Games (since 1936), Asian Games (since 1958) and All Africa Games (since 1965). In the first games in Buenos Aires in 1951, the torch came from Olympia, Greece. Since the 1955 Mexico games, the torch is lit by Aztec people in old temples, first in the Sierra de la Estrella and after in the Temple of the Sun God in the Teotihuacán Pyramids. The only exception was for the São Paulo games in 1963, when the torch was lit in Brasilia by the indigenous Guarani people.

See also

- Parapan American Games

References

[1] "Pan American Sports Games" (http://www.britannica.com/EBchecked/topic/440587/Pan-American-Sports-Games). Encyclopedia Britannica. . Retrieved June 27, 2011.
[2] All time Medals table (http://www.guadalajara2011.org.mx/ENG/02_juegos/resultados_generales.asp)
[3] Medal table History (http://pan.uol.com.br/pan/2007/historia/medalhas.jhtm) (**Portuguese**)
[4] "Pan American Regulation" (http://www.paso-odepa.org/pan_regulations.aspx). *Pan American Sports Organization*. May 27, 2011. .

External links

- Rio 2007 Official Website (http://www.rio2007.org.br/)
- Santo Domingo 2003 Website (http://panamgames2003.com/)
- Pan American Games - Rio de Janeiro 2007 (http://www.quadrodemedalhas.com/en/pan-american-games/pan-american-games-2007-rio-de-janeiro.htm)
- Poster Images from the Pan American Games from 1951 to 1999 (http://www.aafla.org/8saa/PanAm/panam_main.htm)
- Guadalajara 2011 Games (http://www.guadalajara2011.org.mx/esp/index.asp?lng=en)
- Toronto 2015 Games (http://www.toronto2015.org/)

Article Sources and Contributors

Alfredo Valente *Source*: http://en.wikipedia.org/w/index.php?title=Alfredo_Valente *Contributors*: After Midnight, David Gerard, GiantSnowman, Greg Salter, JRRobinson, JonBroxton, Longbomb, Mayumashu, Orlandkurtenbach, R'n'B, Rjwilmsi, Seattlenow, Shotgun pete, Steam5, Zombie433, 1 anonymous edits

Association football *Source*: http://en.wikipedia.org/w/index.php?title=Association_football *Contributors*: 'Arry Boy, 03BTHOMPSON, 05fcrane, 10metreh, 1337B3A57, 144.132.75.xxx, 194.109.232.xxx, 1burke, 1crywolf1, 200120037, 209.20.225.xxx, 21655, 24.218.142.xxx, 24fan24, 2writer, 4019jimmyw, 540dash, 62.253.64.xxx, 62.7.47.xxx, 62.7.5.xxx, 63.192.137.xxx, 84user, A-giau, A.a679100, AEMoreira042281, ARrohetMeZemer, Aabha R, Aaron1716, Abc123youwantme, Aberdeen fc, Abigail-II, Abrech, Abu badali, Academic Challenger, Acalamari, Accurizer, Achinn, AdamWeeden, Adambro, Addshore, Adizlaja, Admrboltz, AdrianTM, Adzeds, Aeon1006, Aeons, Aesopos, Aftesk, Agentknight, AgnosticPreachersKid, Aheyfromhome, Ahills60, Ahoerstemeier, AileanMacRaith, Airconswitch, Aitias, Aj hicks, Ajaxkroon, Akamad, AkdenizliAslan, Aksi great, Aladdinlee, Albinomonkey, Ale jrb, AlefZet, Aleksandr Grigoryev, Alex.muller, Alex43223, Alexis, Alexisamattlover, Alexsh, Alexsoccer102, Alexwiki69, Algebra, Alias Flood, Alsandro, Amalthea, Amazonien, Ambrose222, Ambuj.Saxena, AmiDaniel, AmishThrasher, Amitch, Amorymeltzer, Ams80, AnOddName, AnakngAraw, Anand Bindra, Anaraug, AndeanThunder, Anders Torlind, Anders Törlind, Andocomando, Andonic, Andreasegde, Andres, Andrew Levine, Andrewlp1991, Andries, Andrij Kursetsky, Andrwsc, Andy Marchbanks, Angelo.romano, Angles theatre, Angmering, Angus Lepper, Angusmclellan, Anish9807, Anonywiki, Antandrus, Anthony, Anthonyd3ca, Anyabean17, Aplomado, Aranherunar, Arbor, AriGold, Arnemann, Art LaPella, Arthena, Arthur Holland, Arwel Parry, Asdackla, Ashesdhakal, AshleyMorton, Asmah01, AstroNomer, Astrovega, Atari 667, Athaenara, Atharshiraz, Athomas7990, Attilios, Aubtiger2008, Aude, Auntof6, Australian Matt, Autoerrant, AutomaticWriting, Autonova, Auxil, Avitaltr, Avs5221, Awesome511, AxelBoldt, Aymatth2, Az1568, Azzurro2882, B.Wind, B4hand, BACthegreat, BBJAPS3, BGTopDon, BKH2007, BRG, BUblogger, Babylon32, Baconfish, Badgernet, Bagpuss, Baldhur, Ballboys10, Balthazarduju, Balwan, Bananaman69, Bangaluru, Banhtrung1, Barcafan10, Baristarim, Barliner, BarretBonden, Bart133, Basawala, Basbll4lif23, Baseballbrett13, Bastin, Batman2005, BatteryIncluded, Bawolff, Bbatsell, Bearbug21, Beeman20, Behzad20, Ben davison, Ben-Zin, Ben9dan16, Bender235, Bennelliott, Bennybp, Bento00, Betelgeuse, Beve, Bevo, Bevo74, Bgates456, Biatch, BierHerr, Big Jock Knew, Bigdumbredman2, Bigearedtiger, Bigeazy, Biggieyankfan, Bigpapawaka, Bikeable, BillWSmithJr, Billward, Bkitko, Bkonrad, Blarg000001, Bleakcomb, Bletch, Blokee, Blotsfan, Blue520, Bluelion, Boavi, Bob Palin, Bob schriver, Bob199393, Bob512012, Bobaldinho10, Bobblewik, Bobo192, Bobomg, Bobryuu, Bogdangiusca, Boing! said Zebedee, Bomchickawah, Bongwarrior, Boojanam01, Boole, Borisblue, Bornfury, Bomintheguz, Boshtang, Boychoir, Bozzzzz, Branddobbe, Brandeis, Branko, BreenJnr2@aol.com, Breezeonhold, Brendanurbanwarrior, Brent william mccoy, Brentonf, Brian0918, Brickie, Brighterorange, Brion VIBBER, Brisngr, BritishWatcher, Brod7, Brossow, Bruce1ee, Bryan Derksen, Bryansprang, Bssc81, Btljs, Bubba hotep, Bubbla, Buchanan-Hermit, Bullzeye, Bunnyho1, Bwithh, Byrdman15, ByteofKnowledge, Bz2, C.Fred, C12H22O11, CJ, CPMcE, CS.Aussie, CWii, Cactus.man, Cafzal, Caharayo, CahirAndIrish, Calsicol, Caltas, CambridgeBayWeather, Cameron5dollars, Camerong, Can't sleep, clown will eat me, CanbekEsen, Canek, Canjth, Captain-n00dle, Card Football King, Cardsplayer4life, Carnun, Carreira, Casablanca2000in, Casey56, Casper2k3, Castlecraver, Cataphract, Catch47, CatsClaw, Cbrown1023, Cdc, Cedders, Centrx, Ceoil, Cfarzan, Cfcrowdies18, Cfrydj, Chabby, Chalkwalker, Chandler, Chanheigeorge, CharlieZeb, CharlotteWebb, ChaucerGeoffrey, Checkmate911, Chibinho, Chill doubt, Chillum, Chinesekage, Chingiss, Chkno, Chodorkovskiy, Chris Roy, ChrisTheDude, Chrishatch1973, Chrislk02, Chrism, Christpunkergirl, Chrmb, Chromancer, Chuq, Citizen Premier, Ckatz, Clamster5, Clawed, Clio64B, Clngre, Clocksarecool, Clout, Cls14, Clydecoast, Cmdrjameson, Cncxbox, Cobaltbluetony, Cobaltcigs, Cocoaguy, Code E, Code phil, Codex Sinaiticus, Colin stuart, Colin9brown, Colipon, Collard, Colonies Chris, Commander Shepard, CommonsDelinker, ComputerGuy, Conscious, Conversion script, Cookiva, Coolcaesar, Corean2006, Corvus cornix, Costlab, Counsell, Courtney03, Crafedog, Craig Staples, Craigman0101, Craitman17, Crazycomputers, Crazytales, CreerBFC, Cribananda, Crissov, Cristian Cappiello, Crosstimer, Crystallina, Cs-wolves, CtrlAltDek, Cuchullain, Cuecho, Curps, Custodio.oliveira, Cutler, Cuvette, Cyan, Cybershore, Cyp, DARTH SIDIOUS 2, DB, DGJM, DIEXEL, DJ Clayworth, DVD R W, Da Mastaa, DaGizza, Dachamp724, Dacxjo, Daddy Kindsoul, Daduzi, Daemonic Kangaroo, Daftpunkboy93, Dahliarose, Dale Arnett, Damienhunter, Dan Atkinson, Dan the man 10, DanKeshet, DanRUK, DancingPenguin, Daniel, Daniel Case, Daniel.Cardenas, Daniel5127, Daniel987600, Danlina, Danltn, Danreitz, Dantedanger, Dantheman0056, Dantheman531, Danthemankhan, Daquios, Darkildor, Darkrifle, Darry2385, Darthgriz98, Dave.Dunford, Dave101, Daveb, Davewild, David Johnson, David Levy, David Schaich, Davidbrookesland, Dc19, Ddfree, Deadlock, Deadmanwalking1, Deanh, Debate987, Deeb, Delirium, Delldot, Deltabeignet, Den fjättrade ankan, Dendodge, Denhamd2, DerHexer, Derek Ross, Derild4921, Deus Ex, Didier13, DiegoTristan, Differentgravy, Digitalme, Dijon312, Dim SIM.StPaTs, Dimitrakopulos, Dina, Dinis80654, Dinshoupang, Dirkbb, DirkvdM, Disavian, Discospinster, Disorganized 676, Diving2010, Djdan90, Djln, Djmadd93, Doc glasgow, DocWatson42, Docu, Document, Doglover77, Dojarca, Domcabcd, Donama, Donatj, Donfbreed, Dostal, Doubleslash, Downloadmeh, Dr Santa, Dr31, Dradious, DragonHawk, DragonflySixtyseven, Dragonnas, Draicone, Drmies, Dryazan, Dudesleeper, Duja, Durin, Dust Filter, Dustimagic, Dweller, Dycedarg, DylaHeary, DylanW, EBL, EEMIV, EJF, EPs, ERcheck, ESkog, EWS23, Eagle4000, Earl CG, East718, Ebeisher, Eceresa, Eclecticology, Ed Poor, Ed g2s, EdC, Eddyji999, Edgar181, Eielsonafbman, Einstein100, El Suizo, Elliskev, Emc2, Empty Buffer, Emura, Encephalon, Endroit, Endymi0n, Energyfreezer, Enigmaman, Enoch Wong, Enviroboy, Epsteada, Equazcion, Erath, Ergmuncer, Ericoides, Error, Erzengel, Esanchez7587, Esperant, Estel, Eu.stefan, Evekrogman, Evenmadderjon, Evercat, Everyking, Evice, Evillution, Ewen, Executive.koala, Exploding Boy, Ezeu, Ezhiki, FF2010, Fabian9, Facts707, Fadf, FaerieInGrey, Fainites, Falcon8765, Fan-1967, Fang Aili, Fanta206, Fastily, Fasttimes68, Father Goose, Favonian, FelisLeo, Felix Portier, Fernandopascullo, Feroang, Fewskulchor, Ffahm, Finell, First Light, FisherQueen, Fleagle11, Fliffy, FlipCockle, Floodamanny, Floridan, FluffyWhiteCat, Fluke08, Fmhsxc2010, Fonsildiamond, Fonzy, Football Fan Zone, Footballhead, Footeditor, ForeverWhiteRose, Forshizzle, Foxlarocks, Fr. Jim, Fragbase, Fraggle81, FrancoGG, Frank87, FrankCostanza, Freakofnurture, Fredrik, Freepenguin, FreplySpang, Frischy, Froogoleer, Fruit666, Frymaster, Funandtrvl, Funknl, Funnyfumble5, Fuzzle, Fvasconcellos, Fvw, Fyyer, G-Man, GHoeberX, GVnayR, Gar, Gareth Owen, Garzo, Gaulwiki, Gavinho, Gaw jess, Gazcheung, Gciriani, Gdarin, Gdo01, Gene Nygaard, Geoff janes, Geopersona, George The Dragon, Georgia guy, Gergerballball, German Player, Gerrit, Ghosts&empties, GianniG46, GiantSnowman, Giants2008, Giff1002, Gilesz182, Gilliam, Gilmore Guy, Gilo1969, Gimboid13, Ginajanota, Girlslutgirl, Gizmoleeds, Gkhoyt, Glass Sword, Glen, Globalsolidarity, Gman124, Gnangarra, Gnevin, Goatherd, Gogo Dodo, Gohoos13, Gohoos131, Goldfinger820, Gollumz001, Gooface, Gordongeiger, Grabbies200, Grace Note, GraemeL, GraemeLeggett, Grafen, Graham87, Grant.Alpaugh, Grant65, Green, Greenman, Gregoryj83, Grey Shadow, Gridlock Joe, Griffinofwales, Grm wnr, Grondemar, GroveWanderer, Grover cleveland, Grunners, Gun Powder Ma, Gunray, Gurch, Gwcstcs, Gwernol, Gytrem, Gz33, Hadal, Hadger, Hagerman, Hairchrm, Hairouna, Hairy Dude, Hajima, Haldraper, HalfShadow, Halogeek, Happy2, HappyCamper, Happysailor, Harry Hotspur, Harry Potter, Harry19023, Hashimjaved, Haukurth, Hawkeye7, Hayden5650, Hegemon7786, Heightwatcher, Hemanshu, Henrygb, Hephaestos, Herbert Shek, Herbertxu, Heron, Hesamj, Hesperian, Hflegit16, Hgrenbor, Hi little kids, Hig Hertenfleurst, HighKing, His Ryanness, Hmains, Hockeyplayer371, Hollandfan, Holyjoe, Homer slips., Homestarmy, HomieG2008, Honette, HonorTheKing, Horologium, HungrySphynx2241, Husky, Husond, I already forgot, IJK Principle, INkubusse, Iahead, Iamajpeg, Iamthecutestboyever, Iangibbins, Ichinisan Ilu, Igiffin, Igor, Ihatenyy13, ImperatorExercitus, Imroy, Inhumandecency, Innotata, Intelati, Intellectualfive, Inter16, Interchange88, Iohjasdb, Iota, Iran11, IronGargoyle, Isadera, Isfalk, Itsmine, IvoJovo, Ixfd64, Izelpii, Izno, J Di, J Hofmann Kemp, J.delanoy, JCam, JDDJS, JForget, JFreeman, JHMM13, JIP, JJGD, JLINCON, JNW, JRHorse, JSpudeman, JStewart, JYolkowski, Jacek Kendysz, Jack forbes (renamed), JackieMa, Jackosta1234, Jacoplane, Jacquerie27, Jaffer, Jahiegel, Jake2392, James Foulds, James530, JamesBWatson, JamesMLane, Jamesr@thesportbar.com, Jandrews23jandrews23, Jaranda, Jason Potter, Java13690, Jaxl, Jchild, Jcrow43, Jdawg4820, Jed, Jeff.nolan, Jeff3000, Jennie--x, Jenny4life, JeongHW, JeremyA, Jeronimo, Jersyko, Jesismael, Jesus182, Jfg284, Jhenderson777, Jibbajabba, Jiggelmaster7, Jimfbleak, Jimgawn, Jklin, Jmcc150, Jmed123, Jnestorius, Jni, JoanneB, Joe Cannon Fan, JoeLatics, Joebamber1990, Joebloggsy, Johan Dahlin, Johan Elisson, John, John Anderson, John Reid, JohnOwens, Johnmc, Johnny Jane, Johnnyonthespot, JonBroxton, JonC, JonHarder, Jonik, Jonnysamleland, Jooler, Jor70, Jose77, Joseph Solis in Australia, Joseph Wajsberg, Josh167, Josh619112345267, JoshDuffMan, Josquius, Jossi, Journalist, Joy, Joyous!, Jpogi, Jpollar, Jrdragster11, Jrodes, Jtdirl, Jtkiefer, Ju66l3r, Juancamaney22, Jujutacular, Julia Brewer, Julianp, JuneGloom07, Jusdafax, Jwissick, KIPKIP, Kabillion, Kablammo, Kafziel, Kaihsu, Kaiwhakahaere, Kala25, Kanabekobaton, Karimarie, Karl-Henner, Karmafist, Kathryn NicDhàna, Katieh5584, Kaveh, Kaybull, Kbdank71, Kbh3rd, Keilana, Keith Edkins, Keithdunwoody, KelvSYC, Kenaldinho10, Kernunnos, Kevin B12, Kevin9164, KevinTR, Kevinmon, Kevinzhermin, Keyrocks, Kfitzgib, Khoikhoi, Kidsrus, Kikinou, Kimchi.sg, King Toadsworth, King konger, King of Hearts (old account 2), Kingboyk, Kingjeff, Kingmahad121, Kinigi, Kixix, Kizara, Kizor, Kkm010, Kkornack, Klepto909, Kmccoy, Kneiphof, KnowledgeOfSelf, Kobbra, Kobebryantthejr, Konstable, Kornerkick29, Kosebamse, Kowtoo, Kpalion, Kri, Krich, Kruckenberg.1, KsprayDad, Kubigula, Kukini, Kungfuadam, Kungming2, Kuru, Kurykh, Kwekubo, Kwiki, Kylekyle1, Kylev1, KyraVixen, L Kensington, LSehy, Lacrimosus, Laenfant, Lance181, Landonbrowne, Lardman, Latics, Laughing Man, Laughingirl1515, Lazerburn33, Lazycouch2, Leafyplant, Leandrod, Lectonar, Lee Gregz, LegolasGreenleaf, Leminy, Lemonus, Leon7, Lerdthenerd, Leszek Jańczuk, Liebitz, Liftarn, Lightdarkness, Lightmouse, Lights, Lilcou123, Lilyana, Lindberg, Linkspamremover, Linuxerist, Lion King, Littlechip90, Lkkn, Llcoolspence, Loboxx36, Lofike, LonelyMarble, Lord Hawk, Lord Marco, Lord Voldemort, LordRM, LordSimonofShropshire, Lordkazan, Loren36, Lost4eva, Lotje, Lowercase, Lowzeewee, Lpw, LuFisto, Lucy-marie, Ludraman, LukeSurl, Lumpy joe108, Luna Santin, Lupin, M baptiste, MECU, MER-C, MJCdetroit, MK8, MNAdam, MZMcBride, Mac, Mac Gille Domhnaich, Mac12, MacGyverMagic, Mad sam, MadGeographer, Maday94, Madchester, Madw, Maestro25, Magic in the night, Magister Mathematicae, Magooch2.0, Mah favourite, Mahahahaneapneap, Mahanga, Maihu don, Maitch, Majorly, Malhonen, Malo, Malpass93, Mandel, Maniacgeorge, Maniwar, Manuel11223, Manutd 12345, MapsMan, Marc Venot, Marcika, Marco.spiro, Mareino, Marek69, Marianocecowski, Mark, Mark272, MarkA12, Marrilpet, Marshman, MartinHarper, MartinVillafuerte85, Martingio15, Martyn Smith, Marudubshinki, Master Of Ninja, Masterpjz9, Materialscientist, Mateus RM, Matggggg, Mathnarg, Matiasmoreno, Matt Yeager, Matt r kelly, Matthew R Dunn, Matthewfreile, Mattisse, Matty2002, Mauro100, Mav, Maveric56, Maw, Maxamegalon2000, Maxim, Maximaximax, Maxtin, Mayumashu, Mbecker, McDogm, McKennaMan929, Mcdeans, Mdr2375, Meb83, Meelar, Megan1967, Mendor, Meow1234, Merrettrg01, Methnor, Metropolitan90, Mets501, MetsFan76, Mgaigg, Mglovesfun, Michael (vandal), Michael Hardy, Michael Hawkins, Michael Hinrichs, Michael Johnson, Michael Zimmermann, Michael riber jorgensen, MickMacNee, MickWest, Midgrid, Miguel.mateo, Mike Rosoft, Mike jones gyeah, Mike1, MikeDog94, Mikethechicken, Mikm, Miles Blues, Minesweeper, Minna Sora no Shita, Mintguy, Mirage5000, MisfitToys, Mistakefinder, Mistamagic28, MisterSheik, Misure poo poo, Misza13, Mitsuhirato, Mjfc, Mkamensek, Mmoneypenny, Mmortal03, Mnpeter, MoRsE, Mochachocca, Moeron, Moeyman, Mohammad adil, Monarchius, Money Makers R Us, Monkbel, Monkeyman, Monkeyman11, Mono, Mopyu90, Moravice, Mormegil, Mothani90, Motley Crue Rocks, Mourn, Moyogo, Mr Chuckles, Mr. Bouncy, Mr. G. Williams, MrFish, MrH, MrJanitor1, MrTranscript, Mreult, Mroach12, Mrxcol, Ms2ger, Mshizzi, Mswake, Muchness, Muhammad Mahdi Karim, Mushroom, Mxalienraptor, Mxcatania, Myanw, Mybighead, Mysdaao, Mysekurity, N458jhk1, Nabla, Naddy, Nakon, Nanonic, Narco, Narsamson, Narssarssuaq, Nascar1996, Nath1012, Natjenko, NawlinWiki, Nawsum526, Ncmvocalist, Nebu Pookins, Nedarb0, NeferSnoopy, Neil Leslie, Neiman002, New Vanda1 account!, New World Man, NewEnglandYankee, Newone, Nhilary, Nichalp, Nick, Nick Boulevard, Nick of nickness in Colorado, Nickshanks, Night Gyr, Nihiltres, Nitaro02, Niteowlneils, Nmitbutcher, No Guru, NocturneNoir, Nodoremi, Noeticsage, Noirceuil, Nojika, Nolitafairytale, Nonagonal Spider, Nonforma, Norbutt2001, Northumbrian, Nosskyline, Nrbelex, Nscheffey, Nsh, Nuggets, Num1dgen, Number 57, Nzd, Nzfooty, OLDMAN, Obamafan70, Obli, Ocaasi, Ocrasaroon, Off!, Off2riorob, Ohconfucius, Ohheyyyy, Ohnoitsjamie, Oldelpaso, Oldhamlet, Olivier, Ollytedwards, Olorin28, Omengacarno07, Omglol, Omicronpersei8, On Thermonuclear War, One, OneManDown, OoberMick, Oogadabaga, Orangemaster, Ordinaria, Ortolan88, Ospalh, Othersider, Ouishoebean, Overlord pat, Ownage24, Oxfordwang, Ozbandit, PHDrillSergeant, PIO, Pacheto, Page Up, Pak21, Paleorthid, Palma234@sympatico.ca, Palmiped, Panarjedde, Papitasfritas, Parable1991, Paris 16, Park3r, Parkwells, Pat

Gibson, Patayal, Patchamo123, Patrick, Patrick-br, Paul August, Pb30, Pdcook, Peanut4, PeeJay2K3, Persian Poet Gal, Perstar, Peruvianllama, Pespilaludo, Peter Eedy, Peter Isotalo, Peter S., PeterGrecian, Peterkoning, Peterstannard, Pewwer42, Phantomsnake, Phil Boswell, Philip Baird Shearer, PhilipO, PhilipR, Phillip J, Phobal, Phoenix2, PiRSquared17, Picapica, Pieguy48, PierceCheng, Pilif12p, Pilotboy5, Pilotguy, Pinirice65, Piontek, Pippu d'Angelo, Pit, Pizzaguy4378, Pladask, Plasticup, Plastikspork, Playak, Plm209, Poborak, PoeticVerse, Poindexter Propellerhead, Pokadoteliza, Pol098, Poobslag, Porqin, Portiere 101, Poslanik, PotentialDanger, Poulsen, Powelldinho, Pparazorback, Ppntori, Pratj, PrestonH, Pretty Green, Prewitt81, PrimeCupEevee, Prodego, Pruneau, PseudoSudo, Psveindhoven, Psycho Kirby, Pusht, Python eggs, QAQUAU, Qrc2006, Quadell, Quae legit, QueenCake, Quilker, Quintillion, Quinxorin, QuizQuick, QwerpQwertus, R Lowry, RB972, RHaworth, RJSampson, RPlunk2853, RabidWalrus, Radio Guy, Raelx, Raf45Martinez, Rafaelamonteiro80, Rahuloof, Raichu, Rainjar, Rak-Tai, Ranjithsutari, Rapido, Raul654, Raven4x4x, Ravik, Ray Radlein, Ray7jd, Rd232, Rdikeman, Rdsmith4, Readeraml86, ReadingOldBoy, Recury, Red Director, Redcongocross, Reddi, Redrocketboy, Redshoeszeff, Redsox7897, Redvers, Redwolf24, Reeinstein, Refsworldlee, Regentagger, Reggy123, Reginmund, Regular Daddy, Renegadeviking, Rettetast, Rex the first, RexNL, Reyfan1710, Reywas92, Ricardo Moog, Ricardo monteiro, Rich Farmbrough, Richard Allen, Richard Harvey, Richard Rundle, Rick.G, RickK, Ricky81682, Rickyrab, Rjwilmsi, Rkstafford, Rlynagh-shannon, Rmachenw, Rmhermen, Robdurbar, RobertG, Roberta F., Robertgreer, Robversion1, Robwingfield, Rocket71048576, Rocketboy50, Rogerzilla, Romanm, Ronald Mexico, Rory096, Rosiethegreat, RoyBoy, Royalguard11, Royboycrashfan, Rreagan007, Rulesfan, Rx23xaexstlx, Ryan's mom, Ryan25, Rynne, Ryoissoawesome, Ryulong, S0ccerstud301, S0me l0ser, SAFCjl, SFC9394, SJK, SJP, SM, SMcCandlish, SNIyer12, SQGibbon, Sadettin, Sagz639, Salmon, Salt Yeung, Salvio giuliano, SalvoCalcio, Sam Hocevar, Sam Vimes, Samelchami, Sammyjames, Samsara, Samuel Blanning, SandyGeorgia, Sango123, Sangyerians, SaraBaugh, Sasajid, Sasquatch, Sausage948, Sbluen, Sbrools, Sceptre, SchfiftyThree, Schluum, Schrei, Scienter, Sciurinæ, Scottster03, Sdornan, Sean Whitton, Seanchelsea5, Searlewd, Sebasbronzini, Sebastiankessel, Seglea, Seidenstud, Serein (renamed because of SUL), Serminigo, Serpent-A, Serte, Sethlopez, Sfahey, Sgsilver, Shaddens ate denzel for brekky, Shadowjams, Shaidar cuebiyar, Shanes, Shannon bohle, Shirimasen, Shizhao, Shoemakerenator, Shojeeb, Shortenfs, Shotwell, Shrine of Fire, Shushruth, SidP, Sideshow Bob, Siebren, Sietse Snel, Silence, Silivrenion, SilkTork, Sillyfolkboy, Simba1409, SimonMayer, SimonP, SineWave, Sinteractive, Siqbal, Sir Cumsize, Sir Nicholas de Mimsy-Porpington, SirChan, SirGrant, SirJibby, Sirkad, Sixest, Sjakkalle, Sjorford, Sjö, Skh, Skinnyweed, SkullWeasel, Sky83, Skyler13, Slakr, Slow Graffiti, Sluj, Slumgum, Smart7167126716, Smaug123, Smithsterj, SmthManly, Snarfsnarf, Snipeboy09, Snori, SoCalSuperEagle, SoLando, Soaringbear, Sobolewski, Soccer buff, Soccer plyr66, Soccer219, SoccerNews, Soccerdude, Soccereditor, Soccerkick8, Soccerking11, Soccerman10103, Soccershoes1, Socialsoccer.com, Sofie310, SofiePedersen, Sonjaaa, Soulresin, SouthernNights, SpNeo, Spaniard78, SparqMan, Speed Air Man, Speedy McG, Spencer, SpencerTC, Speshel k, Spewmaster, SpiceMan, Spike Wilbury, Spitzerman, Spliffy, Splintax, Springeragh, SpuriousQ, Spykesinmahshoe, Sq178pv, Squall88, Srose, Ssilvers, St.daniel, Stalfur, Stanrosander, Stanza13, Starcircloco, Starx, Statistic94, Steel, Steers82, Steinan3, Stephen G. Brown, Stephen Parnell, Stephenb, Stepshep, SteveSims, Stevekeiretsu, Stevenhonig, Stevertigo, Stevey7788, Stevo1000, Stockdiver, Stop Climate Change, Struway, Struway2, Stu.W UK, Stui, Stylus Happenstance, Stymphal, Suhalbansal, Suisui, Summerford40, SupaStarGirl, Supadawg, Supplementary, Svick, Swainstonation, Swanyk, Symane, Symon, SynergyBlades, Szater, TFCforever, THUGCHILDz, TLE, TNB774, TRBlom, TSO1D, Taamu, Tad Lincoln, Taemyr, Tainter, TakuyaMurata, Tameamseo, Tanaats, Tancred, Tangerines, Tannin, Tanv91, Tara969, Taroaldo, Tasc, Tata11, Tavix, Tawker, Taylorr, Tbhotch, TeaDrinker, Tedcurly, Tellyaddict, TexMurphy, Thaurisil, The 984, The Anome, The Big C, The Font, The Gnome, The Halo, The Haunted Angel, The Rambling Man, The sock that should not be, The way, the truth, and the light, The wub, TheAmericanizator, TheGrappler, TheProject, Theda, Thefullback, Themodelcitizen, Thenotoriousadin, Therandomthing, Therightclique, Thesoccerjunky4, Thing that goes on feet, Thistle71190, Thryduulf, Thumperward, Thunderboltz, Tiago Heitor, Tibre, TiffaF, TigerShark, Tim R, Timc, Timmc9106, Timrollpickering, Timwi, Tiresais, Titansfan7532, Titoxd, Toby Woodwark, Tocino, Tom harrison, Tom-3124, Tom-3124(back again), TomCat4680, TomPhil, TomasBat, Tony1, TonySt, Tonywalton, Toondude, TootinDaylight, Totsie07, Tpbradbury, Travelbird, Tree Biting Conspiracy, Treed, Trevor MacInnis, Trieste, Trixxy, Trontonian, Trosk, Trouserswonky, Troutrooper, Trovatore, Trusilver, TurboGUY, Tvaughn05, TwoOneTwo, Tyciol, Tyomitch, Uannis, UberCryxic, Ughs, Ultimus, Ultratomio, Un chien andalou, Une fette, Unexplained, Unibond, UnicornTapestry, Unreal7, Uranium grenade, UrbanNerd, Uris, Urzadek, Usergreatpower, Utcursch, Utopial, V111P, VMohanty, Vanjagenije, Vanky, Varitek, Vary, Veed, Vega84, VegaDark, Veinor, Venu62, Vf7993, Viajero, Vidshow, Vikreykja, Vilcxjo, VinceBowdren, Violetriga, Viridae, Viriditas, Vivio Testarossa, Voyagerfan5761, Vrenator, VsD, Vzbs34, W2ch00, WATP, WAvegetarian, WFCforLife, Wackywace, Waggers, Wallerstein, Warfvinge, Warp457, Waseh123321, Wathiik, Wavelength, Wayward, Weregerbil, West coast, Westendgirl, Whall2004, Whatupnathan, Where, Whisky drinker, WhisperToMe, Whouk, Wi-king, Wiki Raja, Wiki alf, Wikibofh, Wikieditor06, Wikien2009, Wikitanvir, Wildnox, Wildplayer61, Will Beback Auto, Willbellum, Willis, Willy on WheeLs, Willy turner, Wingsandsword, Winhunter, Winston365, Wipe, Wknight94, Wmahan, WojPob, Wolfmankurd, WoodenTaco, Woody, Woohookitty, Wrathchild, Wrp103, Wstitans11, Wtmitchell, Wtwilson3, Wutizevrybudylookingat?, Ww2censor, X!, X201, Xanthoxyl, Xaosflux, Xezbeth, Xhack, Xiaodai, Xiner, Xinit, Xornok, Xtra, Xzyilum, Y, Yarnalgo, Yaz0r, Yclept:Berr, Yeahsoo, Yekrats, YellowMonkey, Yoenit, Yonatan, Youndbuckerz, Your soccer boy, Yousou, Ysangkok, Yuckfoo, YuffieTheBear, Zahid Abdassabur, Zanimum, Zaphod Beeblebrox, Zaslav, Zephyr21, ZimZalaBim, Zizouthecat, Zocky, Zolstijers, Zreeon, Zundark, Zytroft, Zzmonty, Zzuuzz, Zzyzx11, [212], Ævar Arnfjörð Bjarmason, Александър, Саша Стефановић, ||ممیری, فرش الدین 3260 anonymous edits

Midfielder *Source*: http://en.wikipedia.org/w/index.php?title=Midfielder *Contributors*: 1223Sallybride, 3E933333Boy, Abu badali, Achangeisasgoodasa, Acmilan10italia, Acmilan224eva, Actionfury199, AdjustShift, Agent Smith (The Matrix), Ajkelvin, Alias Flood, Appraiser, Arthena, Arthur Holland, Awalebede1, Awiseman, Bababoum, Backburner001, Bencherlite, Benjy613, Bergsten, Beve, Bevo74, BishopOcelot, Blackwatch21, Bo yaser, Bobo192, Bobpalloona, Bodnotbod, Boguslavmandzyuk, Bongwarrior, Brave warrior, Brocky9, Bry0392, Bulkroosh, C.Fred, CWFC 02, CalJW, Cbrycey23, Ccfc admin, ChaChaFut, Changyg, CharlesWemyss, Chensiyuan, ChivaRoja, Chris 73, Chris the speller, Chuunen Baka, CieloEstrellado, Citz, Cntras, Coasterlover1994, Cocytus, CommonsDelinker, CorleoneSerpicoMontana, Counsell, Cplusplusian, Crosstimer, Cs-wolves, Csari, Cursive, Cxz111, Cyfal, DARTH SIDIOUS 2, DJ Clayworth, DabMachine, Daemonic Kangaroo, Dale Arnett, Daquios, Dark Mavies, Darkcooler, Dave101, Dead-or-Red, Dedos07, Destiny999, Dh67, Dimitrii, Dndanny, Dodo bird, Dr31, Dragonlord kfb, Dreadstar, Drmies, Dryazan, Duplode, Dwanyewest, ENeville, Earl CG, Efe10, Eixo, Elcien, Elf-friend, Eltricolor, Epbr123, Evanreyes, Exutilizador, Fazman2, Fernandopascullo, Finalius, Flashantenna, Flowerparty, Fwc, Gail Wynand, Gareth E Kegg, Gavin.perch, Ghosts&empties, GilbertoSilvaFan, Gingerdave, Gloryglory, GoldDragon, Grumpyyoungman01, HalfShadow, Halmstad, Hardrada, Hariharan91, Hayabusa future, Hotblaster, Howsaboutno, Hubschrauber729, Husond, Iamtopman, Ian Pitchford, Intelati, Iranway, Iridescent, Italian boy, Ixfd64, JNW, JaGa, Jacek Kendysz, Japa, Jaure10, Jimbo online, Jimmy boy81, JimmyMac82, Joaopais, John, Joy, Juliancolton, K.C. Tang, KCinDC, KairiAkihito, Katelynrocks99, Kerbaby, Kevin9164, Killingthedream, Kinigi, Knarbeh, KnucklesEchidna, Koeilouis, Kookie 4 ever, Kosack, Krun, L Kensington, Lapafrax, LarRan, Lieutenantjamest, LimoWreck, Linhphan22990, Londo06, Lord Shivan, Lorenzinho, Loudsox, LowVelocity, Lucy-marie, M.Kris, MJD86, Mandel, Maniacgeorge, Manop, Marbod Egerius, Mariana Binte Zainal, Marianocecowski, Mark Ekimov, Marznafri, Materialscientist, Mattustaszewski, Maximus Rex, Mbutlerbrown, Me2hero, Mewecleff, Midgey23, Mike Rosoft, Mikhel Pitman, Mirzahasanwaqar, Mojitive, Moriori, Mrdrr, Muchness, Mxcatania, Nasnema, NawlinWiki, Nedzelic, Nick of nickness in Colorado, Nickfraser, Nivix, Nlsanand, Nojika, Nsaa, Oldelpaso, Ondog, Orioane, Ozamoza, Paulromney, PeeJay2K3, Pelmeen10, Philip Trueman, Phósphoros, Pivotal, Pkchan, PokeYourHeadOff, PotentialDanger, Poulsen, Pratj, Psaywer1972, Puffin, QmunkE, Qulqai, Qwghlm, RG2, Ram4eva, Random User 937494, Ravhin, Red star, Rensing, Revolutionfan, Rhe br, Rjwilmsi, Rokkafellah, RonaldoRonaldoRonaldo, Ronhjones, Rulesfan, Rurikbird, Sam Pointon, Scarecroe, Scarfo, Schumi555, Seaphoto, Sebthe1, Setanta747 (locked), Severo, Shadowjams, Shafticus, Shihan07, Sifta88, Sillyfolkboy, SilverVu, Simmo676, SimonMayer, Sir-Nobby, Sirkeg, Skully Collins, Smappy, Smuri, Soccer77, Somali123, Soman, Some jerk on the Internet, Sonic extreme, Sonturin, Sparrowgoose, Spellmaster, Sphallolalia, Stealth.voltage, Stiffknot, Sunderland06, Syphondu, Tech support 451, The Brain of Morbius, The Rambling Man, The Thing That Should Not Be, Thegoz, Thekennethnews, Tide rolls, Tiresais, Tommy2010, Torrasque, Tpth, Transfer, Triumph1500, Trusilver, Typhoonchaser, Ubardak, Ugen64, UnclearWinter, Urdadsleftnipple, Uwabizzle, V4R, Vator08, Veinofstars, Velella, Velvitjester, VicenteRodriguez, Vincent.weil, Vrenator, William.mu, Winston365, Wushugene, X MidnightSon X, XenonWorld, Xman456, Yashiv, Zanneb, Zodiax, 1581 anonymous edits

Alpha Secondary School *Source*: http://en.wikipedia.org/w/index.php?title=Alpha_Secondary_School *Contributors*: Ac1408, Aelfthrytha, Alansohn, Aman606, BazookaJoe, Bearcat, Blehfu, Calabraxthis, Calaka, Can't sleep, clown will eat me, Carinemily, Chubbibunni, Ckatz, Clam0p, Cool-Fly, Discospinster, DoubleBlue, DoubleDuranium123, Ekrubmj, Emarsee, Falvo 8, GWST11, Grishmak, GwaiiEagle, ILovePlankton, Ibanez RYM, JaGa, Jelesi, Ksceric, Makeemlighter, Mrstupper, Mtrayn, Mystylplx, PKT, Pandemoniumexpress, PhilKnight, Piano non troppo, R, Rich Farmbrough, RxELAPSE, Sam Korn, Sanderson 72, Shadowjams, Slappy23645, Snowolf, Steam5, Tassedethe, Tedzsee, TheFeds, Triona, Usgnus, Vianello, Wakemp, Zoobtoob, 150 anonymous edits

Vancouver Whitecaps (1986–2010) *Source*: http://en.wikipedia.org/w/index.php?title=Vancouver_Whitecaps_%281986%E2%80%932010%29 *Contributors*: Acmilan10italia, Admachina, AeonicOmega, After Midnight, Amnoturbegavic, Andrwsc, Ario ManUtd, ArtVandelay13, Auntof6, Balerion, Bearcat, Bernstein2291, Big Smooth, Blackbox77, Bobanny, BobbyAFC, Bobo192, Bouchecl, Bracamonte, Buchanan-Hermit, Burgundavia, Calistemon1, Ccopela3, Chris Edgemon, ChrisCork, Chriswonky, Ckatz, Cliftonian, Cmjc80, Columbian, Coppercanuck, Count de Des Moines, Cptnono, Cs-wolves, Dale Arnett, Dalmond, DamionOWA, Dancreel, Daniel, Dekimasu, Devon Rowcliffe, Differentgravy, Digirami, Dj nix, Djln, Djob, Dkd1, Dr31, Dryazan, Dylant2011, EastVanPete, Ed g2s, Edwinhubbel, Either way, Emarsee, Erpert, Esperanza222, Everard Proudfoot, FF2010, Fennec, Flystraightin, Fratrep, Froztbyte, Gateman1997, Gena Thompson, Ghostreveries, GiantSnowman, Gleorzov Iasnissaoa, GoPurpleNGold24, Grant.Alpaugh, Greg Salter, Gump Stump, Harryzimm, Hede2000, Henryong, Heqs, Hottentotspur, Iam4Lost, Ironfistofanarchy, JRRobinson, Jackyd101, Jcmenal, Jogurney, Johan Elisson, JonBroxton, Juve curr, Kasperone, Katatonic, Kate, Ketiltrout, KitHutch, Lightlowemon, LilHelpa, Loud Mouth Soup, MER-C, Mattythewhite, Mayumashu, Michfan2123, Mikemor92, Mita Otrov, Mohrflies, Monkee102, Morbital, NeilCanada, Nlsanand, Nurmsook, Nutana, Oldtimer6, Otav347, PlppoRotini, Paralympiakos, Paul A, Pharos04, Phreakydancin, Piskku, Puredreamer, Qutezuce, Resolute, Rolando, Sabinb26, Seabear84, Secretlondon, Shootmaster 44, Shotgun pete, Smith03, Spider68, Steam5, TakTak, Tawker, Tedzsee, Tempo21, Thegoz, Tom Danson, TopDogg79, Usgnus, Wac01, Walor, Walter Görlitz, Waterloo1974, Whkoh, Whoneedspants, Wikistoriographer, Ylaaargh, Zackyusoff, Zombie433, Þadius, 330 anonymous edits

Vancouver Metro Soccer League *Source*: http://en.wikipedia.org/w/index.php?title=Vancouver_Metro_Soccer_League *Contributors*: Andrewjgreed, AvicAWB, Bigkhrisdogg, Coppercanuck, Djln, Gateman1997, Gleorzov Iasnissaoa, Mayumashu, N419BH, Tedzsee, ThermoNuclearWar, Truthanado, 8 anonymous edits

Canada men's national under-20 soccer team *Source*: http://en.wikipedia.org/w/index.php?title=Canada_men%27s_national_under-20_soccer_team *Contributors*: Achangeisasgoodasa, Balerion, Bammerz, Boohuboy, Canadasoccer, Canadasoccer1, Chanheigeorge, Chris the speller, Cope0023, Coppercanuck, Cs-wolves, Djln, Dkd1, Dohertypenguin, Gene Nygaard, GiantSnowman, Hammersoft, Hodj222, Jaanusele, Jimbo online, JohnnyPolo24, Jonzo12, JustAGal, Kasperone, LilHelpa, Magog the Ogre, Master Jay, Mayumashu, Mshadeed, NYC2TLV, Number 57, PeeJay2K3, Pitlane02, Quadell, Quentin X, R'n'B, Ratiocinate, Rdroze, Rjwilmsi, Seaphoto, Shootmaster 44, Shotgun pete, Siebrand, Sir-Nobby, TasmaniaUnitedFan, Tassedethe, Thegoz, Themodelcitizen, William Avery, Zombie433, Zondi, 132 anonymous edits

USL First Division *Source*: http://en.wikipedia.org/w/index.php?title=USL_First_Division *Contributors*: -kj, A.K.A.47, A18919, Abdul Qayyum Ahmad, After Midnight, Albinomonkey, Aleksandr Grigoryev, Amerika, Andrwsc, Angr, Anttipng, Automotivado, Azumanga1, Babieboy2786, Bernstein2291, Betacommand, BigT2006, BigrTex, Blackbox77, Bobblehead, BobbyAFC,

Article Sources and Contributors

BoricuaPR, Bornintheguz, Bosteamsrbeast, Brady4mvp, BruB, Bucketsofg, Calsicol, CapitalLetterBeginning, Charruss, Che84, Chivista, Chris Edgemon, Ckatz, Cmjc80, Comayagua99, Coppercanuck, Cougs2000, Crew29, CyMoahk, D Monack, DCUnitedFan2011, Daemonic Kangaroo, Dale Arnett, Dancreel, David Falk, DemonJuice, Digirami, DjIn, Dkd1, Dr31, Dryazan, Duplex13100, ESkog, Eightball, Either way, Ekrubmj, Elliskev, Embele, FJM, Fhurion, FogDevil, Fralambert, Fuzzy510, Gateman1997, Gephart, Gerardo Silva, Ggfgfdhf, Grant.Alpaugh, Greecepwns, Grstain, Gtrojan, Guanako512, Henryong, Hottentotspur, JaMikePA, Jaymillionaire, Jcmenal, Jdmalouff, Jimmy Slade, JohnnyBGood, JohnnyPolo24, JonBroxton, Jonathan97X, Jstein16, JustJuthan, Karataev, Kevin McE, Kevin martinez132, KitHutch, Kitch, KnoxSGT, Kurohone, Largo1965, Lightmouse, Lord Bob, LtPowers, Ltv100, Malpass93, Mayumashu, Megamemnon, Mhking, Mikemor92, Minfo, Mohrflies, Morbital, Movementarian, Ms2ger, Mtndrums, Nate Silva, Newkai, Nfitz, Nick Dillinger, Nick Number, ObiusX, Ohnoitsjamie, Oldtimer6, Ommnomnomgulp, Otav347, Otduff, Paploo, Pcpcpc, Piano non troppo, Plasma Twa 2, Plasticup, Pogo-Pogo-Pogo, Polynova, Rawbeedee, Resolute, RevTenderBranson, Rhino131, Ric36, RobNS, Robocoder, Robster2001, Roh095033, Rreagan007, Scrubzhero, Seabear84, Secretlondon, Shotgun pete, SimonP, Sjorford, Smith03, Soccer fan, Soccerfan321, Soopafred, Spider68, Spikezoft, Stusutcliffe, SunCreator, TFCforever, Tancred, Tascha96, Tassedethe, The Ink Daddy!, Tomagnewemail, Twilight-Brawl, WiJG?, Woody, Woohookitty, Zzyzx11, 417 anonymous edits

2005 United Soccer Leagues *Source*: http://en.wikipedia.org/w/index.php?title=2005_United_Soccer_Leagues *Contributors*: Coppercanuck, DemonJuice, DjIn, Freedom4all, Keith D, Otav347, Resolute, Soccer-holic.

2008 United Soccer Leagues *Source*: http://en.wikipedia.org/w/index.php?title=2008_United_Soccer_Leagues *Contributors*: A18919, Coppercanuck, Daemonic Kangaroo, DemonJuice, DjIn, Dkd1, Fluffernutter, Greecepwns, Ironfistofanarchy, Jeff3000, JonBroxton, Khan singh, Levineps, Michfan2123, Mtndrums, Natedawg519, Nlsanand, Otav347, Quinn 33, Radical Individualist, Rich Farmbrough, Robster2001, Soccer-holic, Theasfl, 21 anonymous edits

2009 United Soccer Leagues *Source*: http://en.wikipedia.org/w/index.php?title=2009_United_Soccer_Leagues *Contributors*: -kj, 777sms, After Midnight, Automotivado, BobbyAFC, BruB, CapPixel, Chapka, Che84, Conti, DemonJuice, Digirami, DjIn, Ekrubmj, Embele, Erik9, Gio1mtl, Grant.Alpaugh, JimboV1, JohnnyPolo24, JonBroxton, Kapoue, Khan singh, Levineps, Mtndrums, Quicksilvre, Soccer-holic, Spider68, Tabletop, Tassedethe, The Ink Daddy!, Tomagnewemail, Twilight-Brawl, WiJG?, Woody, Woohookitty, 87 anonymous edits

Pan American Games *Source*: http://en.wikipedia.org/w/index.php?title=Pan_American_Games *Contributors*: Alpinu, Andres, Andrwsc, Angelo De La Paz, ArielGold, Asterion, AxelBoldt, B1mbo, Bedford, Beland, Beyond My Ken, BigGabriel555, Bill william compton, Bluelion, Bobbyjojo87, Bolivian Unicyclist, BostonRed, Brcosa, Budse, CR85747, Caiaffa, CalgaryWikifan, CanisRufus, Cbradshaw, Chicocvenancio, Citicat, CommonsDelinker, Conphucius, Conscious, DO'Neil, DaveOinSF, David Krysakowski, Djrobgordon, Donarreiskoffer, Edged, Eekerz, Eelamstylez77, Esemono, FAB!AN, Family von stennett, Fawcett5, Felipe Menegaz, Frapoz, Gabbec, Garion96, Gentgeen, Gerardo Campos, Geschichte, GoldDragon, Gorvis, GregorB, Gypsum Miner, High Contrast, Hooperswim, Howcheng, Hu12, Iamcrispydammit, Intoronto1125, J 1982, Jacoplane, Jagged, JamesAM, Jared, Jayron32, Jeronimo, Joao Xavier, Joelr31, Johnny Au, JohnnyB256, Jonas kam, JorgeGG, Juandj, Jwillbur, Kanabekobaton, Kelly Martin, Kesal, Kwamikagami, Leeswoo00, Lomibz, Maikking, Marianocecowski, Mario1996, Markko, MartinVillafuerte85, Maxtremus, Mbell 791983, Mbylinska, Mhking, MiLo28, Mindmatrix, Mohsenkazempur, Montell 74, MrPortuCanada, Mtminchi08, Muhandes, Nalonah, NiteowlneiIs, OhanaUnited, Oliverdp2003, Osplace, PAWiki, Password1125, Paulistanum, Pb30, Pcgomes, Pinnecco, Portalian, PsychoJason, Purgatory Fubar, Quarl, Racepacket, Rd232, Reywas92, Rjwilmsi, Ryanjo, Scraggy4, SeNeKa, Shootmaster 44, Sillyfolkboy, Skyler13, Slakr, SpiffyName, Supaman89, Tadeued, Takkyuu, Tesscass, Trakesht, TurtleMelody, Twice25, WhisperToMe, Whpq, WilyD, Woohookitty, , , 170 anonymous edits

Image Sources, Licenses and Contributors

Image:Alfredo-valente.jpg *Source*: http://en.wikipedia.org/w/index.php?title=File:Alfredo-valente.jpg *License*: Creative Commons Attribution 3.0 *Contributors*: User:Longbomb
File:football iu 1996.jpg *Source*: http://en.wikipedia.org/w/index.php?title=File:Football_iu_1996.jpg *License*: unknown *Contributors*: Attenborough, Avicennasis, Beao, Circeus, Danielk2, Davepape, Herbythyme, J 1982, Juiced lemon, Jusjih, MGA73, Man vyi, Martin H., Ranveig, Rdikeman, Rjt170977, Samleeproductions, Spellcast, Thumperward, Wouterhagens, 23 anonymous edits
File:U20-WorldCup2007-Okotie-Onka edit2.jpg *Source*: http://en.wikipedia.org/w/index.php?title=File:U20-WorldCup2007-Okotie-Onka_edit2.jpg *License*: GNU Free Documentation License *Contributors*: User:Fir0002, User:Nwiebe
File:Soccer goalkeeper.jpg *Source*: http://en.wikipedia.org/w/index.php?title=File:Soccer_goalkeeper.jpg *License*: unknown *Contributors*: U.S. Air Force photo by Master Sgt. Lance Cheung
File:Fußballgeschichte (1872).jpg *Source*: http://en.wikipedia.org/w/index.php?title=File:Fußballgeschichte_(1872).jpg *License*: unknown *Contributors*: Daemonic Kangaroo, Infrogmation, Juiced lemon, Kinigi, Maksim, Man vyi, Pepito, 3 anonymous edits
File:1stRoyalEngineers.png *Source*: http://en.wikipedia.org/w/index.php?title=File:1stRoyalEngineers.png *License*: Public Domain *Contributors*: Ffahm, Responsible?
File:Football pitch metric.svg *Source*: http://en.wikipedia.org/w/index.php?title=File:Football_pitch_metric.svg *License*: Creative Commons Attribution-Sharealike 2.5 *Contributors*: User:NielsF
File:Shunsuke1 20080622.jpg *Source*: http://en.wikipedia.org/w/index.php?title=File:Shunsuke1_20080622.jpg *License*: Creative Commons Attribution-Sharealike 3.0 *Contributors*: User:Neier
Image:Yellow card.svg *Source*: http://en.wikipedia.org/w/index.php?title=File:Yellow_card.svg *License*: Creative Commons Attribution-Sharealike 2.5 *Contributors*: User:ed_g2s
Image:Red card.svg *Source*: http://en.wikipedia.org/w/index.php?title=File:Red_card.svg *License*: Creative Commons Attribution-Sharealike 2.5 *Contributors*: User:ed_g2s
File:Ryan Valentine scores.jpg *Source*: http://en.wikipedia.org/w/index.php?title=File:Ryan_Valentine_scores.jpg *License*: Creative Commons Attribution 2.5 *Contributors*: User:Markbarnes
File:Mecz Polska - Armenia 04 ssj 20070328.jpg *Source*: http://en.wikipedia.org/w/index.php?title=File:Mecz_Polska_-_Armenia_04_ssj_20070328.jpg *License*: GNU Free Documentation License *Contributors*: User:Staszek_Szybki_Jest
File:Cesc Fàbregas Anderson.jpg *Source*: http://en.wikipedia.org/w/index.php?title=File:Cesc_Fàbregas_Anderson.jpg *License*: Creative Commons Attribution 2.0 *Contributors*: Gordon Flood
Image:396px-Boisko PositionsMidfield.png *Source*: http://en.wikipedia.org/w/index.php?title=File:396px-Boisko_PositionsMidfield.png *License*: GNU Free Documentation License *Contributors*: Original uploader was Tiresais at en.wikipedia
Image:396px-Boisko PositionsDMidfield.PNG *Source*: http://en.wikipedia.org/w/index.php?title=File:396px-Boisko_PositionsDMidfield.PNG *License*: Public Domain *Contributors*: Original uploader was Tiresais at en.wikipedia
Image:396px-Boisko PositionsAMidfield.PNG *Source*: http://en.wikipedia.org/w/index.php?title=File:396px-Boisko_PositionsAMidfield.PNG *License*: Public Domain *Contributors*: Original uploader was Tiresais at en.wikipedia
Image:396px-Boisko PositionsWMidfield.PNG *Source*: http://en.wikipedia.org/w/index.php?title=File:396px-Boisko_PositionsWMidfield.PNG *License*: Public Domain *Contributors*: Original uploader was Tiresais at en.wikipedia
Image:Vancouver-Whitecaps-FC-Logo.svg *Source*: http://en.wikipedia.org/w/index.php?title=File:Vancouver-Whitecaps-FC-Logo.svg *License*: unknown *Contributors*: JonBroxton, MBisanz, Morbital, Pharos04, Walter Görlitz
File:Flag of Canada.svg *Source*: http://en.wikipedia.org/w/index.php?title=File:Flag_of_Canada.svg *License*: Public Domain *Contributors*: User:E Pluribus Anthony, User:Mzajac
File:Flag of Iceland.svg *Source*: http://en.wikipedia.org/w/index.php?title=File:Flag_of_Iceland.svg *License*: Public Domain *Contributors*: User:Zscout370, User:Ævar Arnfjörð Bjarmason
Image:86erslogo.png *Source*: http://en.wikipedia.org/w/index.php?title=File:86erslogo.png *License*: unknown *Contributors*: User:After Midnight, User:Cydebot, User:Dj nix, User:Malpass93, User:Morbital, User:OKBot, User:Ohconfucius, User:OsamaK
File:Flag of the United States.svg *Source*: http://en.wikipedia.org/w/index.php?title=File:Flag_of_the_United_States.svg *License*: Public Domain *Contributors*: User:Dbenbenn, User:Indolences, User:Jacobolus, User:Technion, User:Zscout370
File:Flag of Switzerland.svg *Source*: http://en.wikipedia.org/w/index.php?title=File:Flag_of_Switzerland.svg *License*: Public Domain *Contributors*: User:-xfi-, User:Marc Mongenet, User:Zscout370
File:Flag of the Democratic Republic of the Congo.svg *Source*: http://en.wikipedia.org/w/index.php?title=File:Flag_of_the_Democratic_Republic_of_the_Congo.svg *License*: Public Domain *Contributors*: Anime Addict AA, AnonMoos, ChongDae, Denelson83, Ed veg, Fry1989, Future Perfect at Sunrise, Homo lupus, Klemen Kocjancic, LA2, Mattes, Moyogo, Nagy, Neq00, Nightstallion, ThomasPusch, Urhixidur, Vzb83, Wester, Zscout370, 11 anonymous edits
File:Flag of Cameroon.svg *Source*: http://en.wikipedia.org/w/index.php?title=File:Flag_of_Cameroon.svg *License*: Public Domain *Contributors*: (of code)
File:Flag of Ghana.svg *Source*: http://en.wikipedia.org/w/index.php?title=File:Flag_of_Ghana.svg *License*: Public Domain *Contributors*: Benchill, Fry1989, Henswick, Homo lupus, Indolences, Jarekt, Klemen Kocjancic, Neq00, SKopp, ThomasPusch, Threecharlie, Torstein, Zscout370, 4 anonymous edits
File:Flag of Tanzania.svg *Source*: http://en.wikipedia.org/w/index.php?title=File:Flag_of_Tanzania.svg *License*: unknown *Contributors*: User:SKopp
File:Flag of Liberia.svg *Source*: http://en.wikipedia.org/w/index.php?title=File:Flag_of_Liberia.svg *License*: unknown *Contributors*: Government of Liberia
File:Flag of Saint Vincent and the Grenadines.svg *Source*: http://en.wikipedia.org/w/index.php?title=File:Flag_of_Saint_Vincent_and_the_Grenadines.svg *License*: Public Domain *Contributors*: User:SKopp
File:Flag of France.svg *Source*: http://en.wikipedia.org/w/index.php?title=File:Flag_of_France.svg *License*: Public Domain *Contributors*: User:SKopp, User:SKopp, User:SKopp, User:SKopp, User:SKopp, User:SKopp
File:Flag of Jamaica.svg *Source*: http://en.wikipedia.org/w/index.php?title=File:Flag_of_Jamaica.svg *License*: Public Domain *Contributors*: User:Madden
File:Flag of Trinidad and Tobago.svg *Source*: http://en.wikipedia.org/w/index.php?title=File:Flag_of_Trinidad_and_Tobago.svg *License*: Public Domain *Contributors*: AnonMoos, Boricuaeddie, Duduziq, Enbéká, Fry1989, Homo lupus, Klemen Kocjancic, Madden, Mattes, Nagy, Neq00, Nightstallion, Pumbaa80, SKopp, Tomia, 10 anonymous edits
File:Flag of Germany.svg *Source*: http://en.wikipedia.org/w/index.php?title=File:Flag_of_Germany.svg *License*: Public Domain *Contributors*: User:Madden, User:Pumbaa80, User:SKopp
File:Flag of Rhodesia.svg *Source*: http://en.wikipedia.org/w/index.php?title=File:Flag_of_Rhodesia.svg *License*: Public Domain *Contributors*: Sagredo, supersedes image by
File:Flag of Zimbabwe.svg *Source*: http://en.wikipedia.org/w/index.php?title=File:Flag_of_Zimbabwe.svg *License*: Public Domain *Contributors*: User:Madden
File:Flag of Cuba.svg *Source*: http://en.wikipedia.org/w/index.php?title=File:Flag_of_Cuba.svg *License*: Public Domain *Contributors*: see below
File:Flag of Bolivia.svg *Source*: http://en.wikipedia.org/w/index.php?title=File:Flag_of_Bolivia.svg *License*: Public Domain *Contributors*: User:SKopp
File:Flag of Haiti.svg *Source*: http://en.wikipedia.org/w/index.php?title=File:Flag_of_Haiti.svg *License*: unknown *Contributors*: User:Chanheigeorge, User:Denelson83, User:Lokal_Profil, User:Madden, User:Nightstallion, User:Vzb83, User:Zscout370
File:Flag of Bermuda.svg *Source*: http://en.wikipedia.org/w/index.php?title=File:Flag_of_Bermuda.svg *License*: Public Domain *Contributors*: User:Cronholm144, user:Nameneko, user:Nightstallion
File:Flag of Japan.svg *Source*: http://en.wikipedia.org/w/index.php?title=File:Flag_of_Japan.svg *License*: Public Domain *Contributors*: Various
File:Flag of Costa Rica.svg *Source*: http://en.wikipedia.org/w/index.php?title=File:Flag_of_Costa_Rica.svg *License*: Public Domain *Contributors*: User:Gabbe, User:SKopp
File:Flag of England.svg *Source*: http://en.wikipedia.org/w/index.php?title=File:Flag_of_England.svg *License*: Public Domain *Contributors*: User:Nickshanks
Image:Winger mascot.jpg *Source*: http://en.wikipedia.org/w/index.php?title=File:Winger_mascot.jpg *License*: Creative Commons Attribution 3.0 *Contributors*: User:Tedzsee
Image:SOUTHSIDERS.jpg *Source*: http://en.wikipedia.org/w/index.php?title=File:SOUTHSIDERS.jpg *License*: Creative Commons Attribution 3.0 *Contributors*: User:Tedzsee
File:Csa logo.png *Source*: http://en.wikipedia.org/w/index.php?title=File:Csa_logo.png *License*: unknown *Contributors*: Angelo.romano, BigrTex, Billybobalobadob, Dj nix, Hammersoft, Lexicon, Melesse, Nfitz, Shootmaster 44, Tbhotch, Tedzsee
File:Flag of Mexico.svg *Source*: http://en.wikipedia.org/w/index.php?title=File:Flag_of_Mexico.svg *License*: Public Domain *Contributors*: User:AlexCovarrubias
File:Flag of the Dominican Republic.svg *Source*: http://en.wikipedia.org/w/index.php?title=File:Flag_of_the_Dominican_Republic.svg *License*: Public Domain *Contributors*: User:Nightstallion
File:Flag of Niger.svg *Source*: http://en.wikipedia.org/w/index.php?title=File:Flag_of_Niger.svg *License*: Public Domain *Contributors*: User:verdy_p

Image Sources, Licenses and Contributors

File:Flag of Italy.svg *Source*: http://en.wikipedia.org/w/index.php?title=File:Flag_of_Italy.svg *License*: Public Domain *Contributors*: see below
File:Flag of the Czech Republic.svg *Source*: http://en.wikipedia.org/w/index.php?title=File:Flag_of_the_Czech_Republic.svg *License*: Public Domain *Contributors*: special commission (of code) SVG version by cs:-xfi-. Colors according to Appendix No. 3 of czech legal Act 3/1993. cs:Zirland.
File:Flag of Wales 2.svg *Source*: http://en.wikipedia.org/w/index.php?title=File:Flag_of_Wales_2.svg *License*: Public Domain *Contributors*: AlexD, Cecil, Dbenbenn, Duduziq, F. F. Fjodor, FruitMonkey, Fry1989, Homo lupus, Iago4096, Pumbaa80, Red devil 666, Srtxg, Torstein, Vernanimalcula, Vzb83, Wouterhagens, 4 anonymous edits
File:Flag of Scotland.svg *Source*: http://en.wikipedia.org/w/index.php?title=File:Flag_of_Scotland.svg *License*: Public Domain *Contributors*: User:Kbolino
File:Flag of Argentina.svg *Source*: http://en.wikipedia.org/w/index.php?title=File:Flag_of_Argentina.svg *License*: Public Domain *Contributors*: User:Dbenbenn
File:Flag of Portugal.svg *Source*: http://en.wikipedia.org/w/index.php?title=File:Flag_of_Portugal.svg *License*: Public Domain *Contributors*: User:Nightstallion
File:Flag of Tunisia.svg *Source*: http://en.wikipedia.org/w/index.php?title=File:Flag_of_Tunisia.svg *License*: Public Domain *Contributors*: AnonMoos, Avala, Bender235, Duduziq, Elina2308, Emmanuel.boutet, Flad, Fry1989, Gabbe, Juiced lemon, Klemen Kocjancic, Mattes, Meno25, Moumou82, Myself488, Neq00, Nightstallion, Reisio, Str4nd, TFCforever, Ö, Фёдор Гусляров, 8 anonymous edits
File:Flag of Australia.svg *Source*: http://en.wikipedia.org/w/index.php?title=File:Flag_of_Australia.svg *License*: Public Domain *Contributors*: Ian Fieggen
File:Flag of the Soviet Union.svg *Source*: http://en.wikipedia.org/w/index.php?title=File:Flag_of_the_Soviet_Union.svg *License*: Public Domain *Contributors*: A1, Ahmadi, Alex Smotrov, Alvis Jean, Art-top, BagnoHax, Denniss, ELeschev, EugeneZelenko, F l a n k e r, Fred J, Fry1989, G.dallorto, Garynysmon, Herbythyme, Homo lupus, Jake Wartenberg, MaggotMaster, Ms2ger, Nightstallion, Pianist, R-41, Rainforest tropicana, Sebyugez, Solbris, Storkk, Str4nd, Tabasco, ThomasPusch, Toben, Twilight Chill, Xgeorg, Zscout370, Серп, 55 anonymous edits
File:Flag of Chile.svg *Source*: http://en.wikipedia.org/w/index.php?title=File:Flag_of_Chile.svg *License*: Public Domain *Contributors*: User:SKopp
File:Flag of Saudi Arabia.svg *Source*: http://en.wikipedia.org/w/index.php?title=File:Flag_of_Saudi_Arabia.svg *License*: Public Domain *Contributors*: Unknown
File:Flag of Qatar.svg *Source*: http://en.wikipedia.org/w/index.php?title=File:Flag_of_Qatar.svg *License*: Public Domain *Contributors*: (of code)
File:Flag of Malaysia.svg *Source*: http://en.wikipedia.org/w/index.php?title=File:Flag_of_Malaysia.svg *License*: Public Domain *Contributors*: User:SKopp
File:Flag of Nigeria.svg *Source*: http://en.wikipedia.org/w/index.php?title=File:Flag_of_Nigeria.svg *License*: Public Domain *Contributors*: User:Jhs
File:Flag of the United Arab Emirates.svg *Source*: http://en.wikipedia.org/w/index.php?title=File:Flag_of_the_United_Arab_Emirates.svg *License*: Public Domain *Contributors*: Anime Addict AA, Avala, Dbenbenn, Duduziq, F l a n k e r, Fry1989, Fukaumi, Gryffindor, Guanaco, Homo lupus, Kacir, Klemen Kocjancic, Krun, Madden, Neq00, Nightstallion, Piccadilly Circus, Pmsyyz, RamzyAbueita, 4 anonymous edits
File:Flag of the Netherlands.svg *Source*: http://en.wikipedia.org/w/index.php?title=File:Flag_of_the_Netherlands.svg *License*: Public Domain *Contributors*: User:Zscout370
File:Flag of Egypt.svg *Source*: http://en.wikipedia.org/w/index.php?title=File:Flag_of_Egypt.svg *License*: Public Domain *Contributors*: Open Clip Art
File:USL First Division.png *Source*: http://en.wikipedia.org/w/index.php?title=File:USL_First_Division.png *License*: unknown *Contributors*: User:Angelo.romano, User:Bernstein2291, User:BetacommandBot, User:Cydebot, User:DerHexer, User:Dryazan, User:Polbot, User:SeventyThree
File:Flag of Puerto Rico.svg *Source*: http://en.wikipedia.org/w/index.php?title=File:Flag_of_Puerto_Rico.svg *License*: Public Domain *Contributors*: User:Madden
file:USA location map.svg *Source*: http://en.wikipedia.org/w/index.php?title=File:USA_location_map.svg *License*: Creative Commons Attribution-Sharealike 3.0 *Contributors*: User:NordNordWest
File:red_pog.svg *Source*: http://en.wikipedia.org/w/index.php?title=File:Red_pog.svg *License*: Public Domain *Contributors*: User:Andux
File:green_pog.svg *Source*: http://en.wikipedia.org/w/index.php?title=File:Green_pog.svg *License*: Public Domain *Contributors*: Andux, Antonsusi, Juiced lemon, Rocket000, STyx, TwoWings, Wouterhagens, 3 anonymous edits
File:Soccerball shade.svg *Source*: http://en.wikipedia.org/w/index.php?title=File:Soccerball_shade.svg *License*: Public Domain *Contributors*: User:Ed g2s
Image:Flag of PASO.svg *Source*: http://en.wikipedia.org/w/index.php?title=File:Flag_of_PASO.svg *License*: Public Domain *Contributors*: B1mbo, 2 anonymous edits
File:Pan American Games host countries.png *Source*: http://en.wikipedia.org/w/index.php?title=File:Pan_American_Games_host_countries.png *License*: Creative Commons Attribution-Sharealike 3.0 *Contributors*: User:Bill william compton
File:Flag of Mexico (1934-1968).svg *Source*: http://en.wikipedia.org/w/index.php?title=File:Flag_of_Mexico_(1934-1968).svg *License*: Public Domain *Contributors*: TownDown
File:US flag 49 stars.svg *Source*: http://en.wikipedia.org/w/index.php?title=File:US_flag_49_stars.svg *License*: Public Domain *Contributors*: Flag design by the U.S. Government; SVG created by w:user:jacobolusjacobolus using w:Adobe IllustratorAdobe Illustrator, and released into the public domain
File:Flag of Brazil (1960-1968).svg *Source*: http://en.wikipedia.org/w/index.php?title=File:Flag_of_Brazil_(1960-1968).svg *License*: Public Domain *Contributors*: Fry1989, Guilherme Paula, Homo lupus, Infrogmation, J.delanoy, Jarekt, Kallerna, Pixeltoo, TigerTjäder, Xufanc, 9 anonymous edits
File:Flag of Colombia.svg *Source*: http://en.wikipedia.org/w/index.php?title=File:Flag_of_Colombia.svg *License*: Public Domain *Contributors*: User:SKopp
File:Flag of Puerto Rico (1952-1995).svg *Source*: http://en.wikipedia.org/w/index.php?title=File:Flag_of_Puerto_Rico_(1952-1995).svg *License*: Public Domain *Contributors*: User:Madden, User:Madden
File:Flag of Venezuela 1930-2006.svg *Source*: http://en.wikipedia.org/w/index.php?title=File:Flag_of_Venezuela_1930-2006.svg *License*: Public Domain *Contributors*: B1mbo, CHV, Denelson83, Gabbe, Homo lupus, Huhsunqu, Micheletb, Mikko Paananen, Reisio, SeNeKa, TFCforever, Wereon, Zscout370
File:Flag of Brazil.svg *Source*: http://en.wikipedia.org/w/index.php?title=File:Flag_of_Brazil.svg *License*: Public Domain *Contributors*: Brazilian Government
File:Flag of Venezuela.svg *Source*: http://en.wikipedia.org/w/index.php?title=File:Flag_of_Venezuela.svg *License*: Public Domain *Contributors*: Bastique, Denelson83, DerFussi, Fry1989, George McFinnigan, Herbythyme, Homo lupus, Huhsunqu, Infrogmation, Klemen Kocjancic, Ludger1961, Neq00, Nightstallion, Reisio, ThomasPusch, Vzb83, Wikisole, Zscout370, 12 anonymous edits
File:Flag of Ecuador.svg *Source*: http://en.wikipedia.org/w/index.php?title=File:Flag_of_Ecuador.svg *License*: Public Domain *Contributors*: President of the Republic of Ecuador, Zscout370
File:Flag of Uruguay.svg *Source*: http://en.wikipedia.org/w/index.php?title=File:Flag_of_Uruguay.svg *License*: Public Domain *Contributors*: CommonsDelinker, Fry1989, Homo lupus, Huhsunqu, Kineto007, Klemen Kocjancic, Kookaburra, Lorakesz, Mattes, Neq00, Nightstallion, Pumbaa80, Reisio, ThomasPusch, Zscout370, , 7 anonymous edits
File:Flag of Guatemala.svg *Source*: http://en.wikipedia.org/w/index.php?title=File:Flag_of_Guatemala.svg *License*: Public Domain *Contributors*: User:Denelson83, User:Vzb83
File:Flag of the Bahamas.svg *Source*: http://en.wikipedia.org/w/index.php?title=File:Flag_of_the_Bahamas.svg *License*: Public Domain *Contributors*: Bahamas government
File:Flag of Peru.svg *Source*: http://en.wikipedia.org/w/index.php?title=File:Flag_of_Peru.svg *License*: Public Domain *Contributors*: User:Dbenbenn
File:Flag of the Netherlands Antilles.svg *Source*: http://en.wikipedia.org/w/index.php?title=File:Flag_of_the_Netherlands_Antilles.svg *License*: Public Domain *Contributors*: Denelson83, Duduziq, Fry1989, Homo lupus, Mattes, Nightstallion, Pumbaa80, TFCforever, Zscout370, 1 anonymous edits
File:Flag of Panama.svg *Source*: http://en.wikipedia.org/w/index.php?title=File:Flag_of_Panama.svg *License*: Public Domain *Contributors*: -xfi-, Addicted04, Duduziq, Fadi the philologer, Fry1989, Klemen Kocjancic, Liftarn, Mattes, Nightstallion, Ninane, Pumbaa80, Reisio, Rfc1394, TFCforever, Thomas81, ThomasPusch, Zscout370, Ö, Фёдор Гусляров, 17 anonymous edits
File:Flag of Suriname.svg *Source*: http://en.wikipedia.org/w/index.php?title=File:Flag_of_Suriname.svg *License*: Public Domain *Contributors*: ALE!, Anime Addict AA, Fry1989, Homo lupus, Klemen Kocjancic, Kookaburra, Krun, Mattes, Mikewazhere, Mmxx, Nightstallion, Pfctdayelise, Reisio, ThomasPusch, Vzb83, Zscout370, 16 anonymous edits
File:Flag of Guyana.svg *Source*: http://en.wikipedia.org/w/index.php?title=File:Flag_of_Guyana.svg *License*: Public Domain *Contributors*: User:SKopp
File:Flag of El Salvador.svg *Source*: http://en.wikipedia.org/w/index.php?title=File:Flag_of_El_Salvador.svg *License*: Public Domain *Contributors*: user:Nightstallion
File:Flag of Antigua and Barbuda.svg *Source*: http://en.wikipedia.org/w/index.php?title=File:Flag_of_Antigua_and_Barbuda.svg *License*: Public Domain *Contributors*: User:Dbenbenn
File:Flag of Nicaragua.svg *Source*: http://en.wikipedia.org/w/index.php?title=File:Flag_of_Nicaragua.svg *License*: Public Domain *Contributors*: User:Nightstallion
File:Flag of the United States Virgin Islands.svg *Source*: http://en.wikipedia.org/w/index.php?title=File:Flag_of_the_United_States_Virgin_Islands.svg *License*: Public Domain *Contributors*: User:Dbenbenn
File:Flag of Barbados.svg *Source*: http://en.wikipedia.org/w/index.php?title=File:Flag_of_Barbados.svg *License*: Public Domain *Contributors*: User:Denelson83
File:Flag of the Cayman Islands.svg *Source*: http://en.wikipedia.org/w/index.php?title=File:Flag_of_the_Cayman_Islands.svg *License*: Public Domain *Contributors*: Collard, Denelson83, Duduziq, Finavon, Fry1989, Guy0307, Krun, Lokal Profil, Mattes, Neq00, Nightstallion, Theda, Zscout370, 7 anonymous edits
File:Flag of Honduras.svg *Source*: http://en.wikipedia.org/w/index.php?title=File:Flag_of_Honduras.svg *License*: Public Domain *Contributors*: D1990, Denelson83, ECanalla, Feydey, Fred J, Homo lupus, Klemen Kocjancic, Mattes, Matthew hk, Neq00, Oak27, Pumbaa80, Rocket000, RubiksMaster110, SKopp, ThomasPusch, Tocino, Vzb83, Yuval Madar, ZooFari, Zscout370, 10 anonymous edits
File:Flag of Paraguay.svg *Source*: http://en.wikipedia.org/w/index.php?title=File:Flag_of_Paraguay.svg *License*: Public Domain *Contributors*: Republica del Paraguay
File:Flag of Grenada.svg *Source*: http://en.wikipedia.org/w/index.php?title=File:Flag_of_Grenada.svg *License*: Public Domain *Contributors*: User:SKopp

Image Sources, Licenses and Contributors

File:Flag of Dominica.svg *Source*: http://en.wikipedia.org/w/index.php?title=File:Flag_of_Dominica.svg *License*: Public Domain *Contributors*: User:Nightstallion

File:Flag of Belize.svg *Source*: http://en.wikipedia.org/w/index.php?title=File:Flag_of_Belize.svg *License*: Public Domain *Contributors*: Caleb Moore

File:Flag of Saint Lucia.svg *Source*: http://en.wikipedia.org/w/index.php?title=File:Flag_of_Saint_Lucia.svg *License*: Public Domain *Contributors*: User:SKopp

File:Flag of Saint Kitts and Nevis.svg *Source*: http://en.wikipedia.org/w/index.php?title=File:Flag_of_Saint_Kitts_and_Nevis.svg *License*: Public Domain *Contributors*: User:Pumbaa80

File:Flag of Aruba.svg *Source*: http://en.wikipedia.org/w/index.php?title=File:Flag_of_Aruba.svg *License*: Public Domain *Contributors*: Anime Addict AA, ChongDae, Duduziq, Enbéká, Fry1989, Homo lupus, Mattes, Moipaulochon, Neq00, TFCforever, Vzb83, Wester, Zscout370

File:Flag of the British Virgin Islands.svg *Source*: http://en.wikipedia.org/w/index.php?title=File:Flag_of_the_British_Virgin_Islands.svg *License*: Public Domain *Contributors*: CeleritasSoni, Cäsium137, Dbenbenn, Denelson83, DenghiùComm, Denniss, Duduziq, Eugenio Hansen, OFS, Fry1989, Homo lupus, Ludger1961, Mattes, Neq00, Nightstallion, Xenophon, 2 anonymous edits

License

Creative Commons Attribution-ShareAlike 3.0 Unported - Deed

This is a human-readable summary of the Creative Commons Attribution ShareAlike 3.0 Unported License (http://en.wikipedia.org/wiki/Wikipedia:Text_of_Creative_Commons_Attribution-ShareAlike_3.0_Unported_License)

You are free:

- **to Share**—to copy, distribute and transmit the work, and
- **to Remix**—to adapt the work

Under the following conditions:

- **Attribution**—You must attribute the work in the manner specified by the author or licensor (but not in any way that suggests that they endorse you or your use of the work.)
- **Share Alike**—If you alter, transform, or build upon this work, you may distribute the resulting work only under the same, similar or a compatible license.

With the understanding that:

- **Waiver**—Any of the above conditions can be waived if you get permission from the copyright holder.
- **Other Rights**—In no way are any of the following rights affected by the license:
  - your fair dealing or fair use rights;
  - the author's moral rights; and
  - rights other persons may have either in the work itself or in how the work is used, such as publicity or privacy rights.
- **Notice**—For any reuse or distribution, you must make clear to others the license terms of this work. The best way to do that is with a link to http://creativecommons.org/licenses/by-sa/3.0/

GNU Free Documentation License

As of July 15, 2009 Wikipedia has moved to a dual-licensing system that supersedes the previous GFDL only licensing. In short, this means that text licensed under the GFDL can no longer be imported to Wikipedia. Additionally, text contributed after that date can not be exported under the GFDL license. See Wikipedia:Licensing update for further information.

Version 1.3, 3 November 2008 Copyright (C) 2000, 2001, 2002, 2007, 2008 Free Software Foundation, Inc. <http://fsf.org/>

Everyone is permitted to copy and distribute verbatim copies of this license document, but changing it is not allowed.

0. PREAMBLE

The purpose of this License is to make a manual, textbook, or other functional and useful document "free" in the sense of freedom: to assure everyone the effective freedom to copy and redistribute it, with or without modifying it, either commercially or noncommercially. Secondarily, this License preserves for the author and publisher a way to get credit for their work, while not being considered responsible for modifications made by others.

This License is a kind of "copyleft", which means that derivative works of the document must themselves be free in the same sense. It complements the GNU General Public License, which is a copyleft license designed for free software.

We have designed this License in order to use it for manuals for free software, because free software needs free documentation: a free program should come with manuals providing the same freedoms that the software does. But this License is not limited to software manuals; it can be used for any textual work, regardless of subject matter or whether it is published as a printed book. We recommend this License principally for works whose purpose is instruction or reference.

1. APPLICABILITY AND DEFINITIONS

This License applies to any manual or other work, in any medium, that contains a notice placed by the copyright holder saying it can be distributed under the terms of this License. Such a notice grants a world-wide, royalty-free license, unlimited in duration, to use that work under the conditions stated herein. The "Document", below, refers to any such manual or work. Any member of the public is a licensee, and is addressed as "you". You accept the license if you copy, modify or distribute the work in a way requiring permission under copyright law.

A "Modified Version" of the Document means any work containing the Document or a portion of it, either copied verbatim, or with modifications and/or translated into another language.

A "Secondary Section" is a named appendix or a front-matter section of the Document that deals exclusively with the relationship of the publishers or authors of the Document to the Document's overall subject (or to related matters) and contains nothing that could fall directly within that overall subject. (Thus, if the Document is in part a textbook of mathematics, a Secondary Section may not explain any mathematics.) The relationship could be a matter of historical connection with the subject or with related matters, or of legal, commercial, philosophical, ethical or political position regarding them.

The "Invariant Sections" are certain Secondary Sections whose titles are designated, as being those of Invariant Sections, in the notice that says that the Document is released under this License. If a section does not fit the above definition of Secondary then it is not allowed to be designated as Invariant. The Document may contain zero Invariant Sections. If the Document does not identify any Invariant Sections then there are none.

The "Cover Texts" are certain short passages of text that are listed, as Front-Cover Texts or Back-Cover Texts, in the notice that says that the Document is released under this License. A Front-Cover Text may be at most 5 words, and a Back-Cover Text may be at most 25 words.

A "Transparent" copy of the Document means a machine-readable copy, represented in a format whose specification is available to the general public, that is suitable for revising the document straightforwardly with generic text editors or (for images composed of pixels) generic paint programs or (for drawings) some widely available drawing editor, and that is suitable for input to text formatters or for automatic translation to a variety of formats suitable for input to text formatters. A copy made in an otherwise Transparent file format whose markup, or absence of markup, has been arranged to thwart or discourage subsequent modification by readers is not Transparent. An image format is not Transparent if used for any substantial amount of text. A copy that is not "Transparent" is called "Opaque".

Examples of suitable formats for Transparent copies include plain ASCII without markup, Texinfo input format, LaTeX input format, SGML or XML using a publicly available DTD, and standard-conforming simple HTML, PostScript or PDF designed for human modification. Examples of transparent image formats include PNG, XCF and JPG. Opaque formats include proprietary formats that can be read and edited only by proprietary word processors, SGML or XML for which the DTD and/or processing tools are not generally available, and the machine-generated HTML, PostScript or PDF produced by some word processors for output purposes only.

The "Title Page" means, for a printed book, the title page itself, plus such following pages as are needed to hold, legibly, the material this License requires to appear in the title page. For works in formats which do not have any title page as such, "Title Page" means the text near the most prominent appearance of the work's title, preceding the beginning of the body of the text.

The "publisher" means any person or entity that distributes copies of the Document to the public.

A section "Entitled XYZ" means a named subunit of the Document whose title either is precisely XYZ or contains XYZ in parentheses following text that translates XYZ in another language. (Here XYZ stands for a specific section name mentioned below, such as "Acknowledgements", "Dedications", "Endorsements", or "History".) To "Preserve the Title" of such a section when you modify the Document means that it remains a section "Entitled XYZ" according to this definition.

The Document may include Warranty Disclaimers next to the notice which states that this License applies to the Document. These Warranty Disclaimers are considered to be included by reference in this License, but only as regards disclaiming warranties: any other implication that these Warranty Disclaimers may have is void and has no effect on the meaning of this License.

2. VERBATIM COPYING

You may copy and distribute the Document in any medium, either commercially or noncommercially, provided that this License, the copyright notices, and the license notice saying this License applies to the Document are reproduced in all copies, and that you add no other conditions whatsoever to those of this License. You may not use technical measures to obstruct or control the reading or further copying of the copies you make or distribute. However, you may accept compensation in exchange for copies. If you distribute a large enough number of copies you must also follow the conditions in section 3.

You may also lend copies, under the same conditions stated above, and you may publicly display copies.

3. COPYING IN QUANTITY

If you publish printed copies (or copies in media that commonly have printed covers) of the Document, numbering more than 100, and the Document's license notice requires Cover Texts, you must enclose the copies in covers that carry, clearly and legibly, all these Cover Texts: Front-Cover Texts on the front cover, and Back-Cover Texts on the back cover. Both covers must also clearly and legibly identify you as the publisher of these copies. The front cover must present the full title with all words of the title equally prominent and visible. You may add other material on the covers in addition. Copying with changes limited to the covers, as long as they preserve the title of the Document and satisfy these conditions, can be treated as verbatim copying in other respects.

If the required texts for either cover are too voluminous to fit legibly, you should put the first ones listed (as many as fit reasonably) on the actual cover, and continue the rest onto adjacent pages.

If you publish or distribute Opaque copies of the Document numbering more than 100, you must either include a machine-readable Transparent copy along with each Opaque copy, or state in or with each Opaque copy a computer-network location from which the general network-using public has access to download using public-standard network protocols a complete Transparent copy of the Document, free of added material. If you use the latter option, you must take reasonably prudent steps, when you begin distribution of Opaque copies in quantity, to ensure that this Transparent copy will remain thus accessible at the stated location until at least one year after the last time you distribute an Opaque copy (directly or through your agents or retailers) of that edition to the public.

It is requested, but not required, that you contact the authors of the Document well before redistributing any large number of copies, to give them a chance to provide you with an updated version of the Document.

4. MODIFICATIONS

You may copy and distribute a Modified Version of the Document under the conditions of sections 2 and 3 above, provided that you release the Modified Version under precisely this License, with the Modified Version filling the role of the Document, thus licensing distribution and modification of the Modified Version to whoever possesses a copy of it. In addition, you must do these things in the Modified Version:

A. Use in the Title Page (and on the covers, if any) a title distinct from that of the Document, and from those of previous versions (which should, if there were any, be listed in the History section of the Document). You may use the same title as a previous version if the original publisher of that version gives permission.
B. List on the Title Page, as authors, one or more persons or entities responsible for authorship of the modifications in the Modified Version, together with at least five of the principal authors of the Document (all of its principal authors, if it has fewer than five), unless they release you from this requirement.
C. State on the Title page the name of the publisher of the Modified Version, as the publisher.
D. Preserve all the copyright notices of the Document.
E. Add an appropriate copyright notice for your modifications adjacent to the other copyright notices.
F. Include, immediately after the copyright notices, a license notice giving the public permission to use the Modified Version under the terms of this License, in the form shown in the Addendum below.
G. Preserve in that license notice the full lists of Invariant Sections and required Cover Texts given in the Document's license notice.
H. Include an unaltered copy of this License.
I. Preserve the section Entitled "History", Preserve its Title, and add to it an item stating at least the title, year, new authors, and publisher of the Modified Version as given on the Title Page. If there is no section Entitled "History" in the Document, create one stating the title, year, authors, and publisher of the Document as given on its Title Page, then add an item describing the Modified Version as stated in the previous sentence.
J. Preserve the network location, if any, given in the Document for public access to a Transparent copy of the Document, and likewise the network locations given in the Document for previous versions it was based on. These may be placed in the "History" section. You may omit a network location for a work that was published at least four years before the Document itself, or if the original publisher of the version it refers to gives permission.
K. For any section Entitled "Acknowledgements" or "Dedications", Preserve the Title of the section, and preserve in the section all the substance and tone of each of the contributor acknowledgements and/or dedications given therein.
L. Preserve all the Invariant Sections of the Document, unaltered in their text and in their titles. Section numbers or the equivalent are not considered part of the section titles.
M. Delete any section Entitled "Endorsements". Such a section may not be included in the Modified Version.
N. Do not retitle any existing section to be Entitled "Endorsements" or to conflict in title with any Invariant Section.
O. Preserve any Warranty Disclaimers.

If the Modified Version includes new front-matter sections or appendices that qualify as Secondary Sections and contain no material copied from the Document, you may at your option designate some or all of these sections as invariant. To do this, add their titles to the list of Invariant Sections in the Modified Version's license notice. These titles must be distinct from any other section titles.

You may add a section Entitled "Endorsements", provided it contains nothing but endorsements of your Modified Version by various parties—for example, statements of peer review or that the text has been approved by an organization as the authoritative definition of a standard.

You may add a passage of up to five words as a Front-Cover Text, and a passage of up to 25 words as a Back-Cover Text, to the end of the list of Cover Texts in the Modified Version. Only one passage of Front-Cover Text and one of Back-Cover Text may be added by (or through arrangements made by) any one entity. If the Document already includes a cover text for the same cover, previously added by you or by arrangement made by the same entity you are acting on behalf of, you may not add another; but you may replace the old one, on explicit permission from the previous publisher that added the old one.

The author(s) and publisher(s) of the Document do not by this License give permission to use their names for publicity for or to assert or imply endorsement of any Modified Version.

5. COMBINING DOCUMENTS

You may combine the Document with other documents released under this License, under the terms defined in section 4 above for modified versions, provided that you include in the combination all of the Invariant Sections of all of the original documents, unmodified, and list them all as Invariant Sections of your combined work in its license notice, and that you preserve all their Warranty Disclaimers.

The combined work need only contain one copy of this License, and multiple identical Invariant Sections may be replaced with a single copy. If there are multiple Invariant Sections with the same name but different contents, make the title of each such section unique by adding at the end of it, in parentheses, the name of the original author or publisher of that section if known, or else a unique number. Make the same adjustment to the section titles in the list of Invariant Sections in the license notice of the combined work.

In the combination, you must combine any sections Entitled "History" in the various original documents, forming one section Entitled "History"; likewise combine any sections Entitled "Acknowledgements", and any sections Entitled "Dedications". You must delete all sections Entitled "Endorsements".

6. COLLECTIONS OF DOCUMENTS

You may make a collection consisting of the Document and other documents released under this License, and replace the individual copies of this License in the various documents with a single copy that is included in the collection, provided that you follow the rules of this License for verbatim copying of each of the documents in all other respects.

You may extract a single document from such a collection, and distribute it individually under this License, provided you insert a copy of this License into the extracted document, and follow this License in all other respects regarding verbatim copying of that document.

7. AGGREGATION WITH INDEPENDENT WORKS

A compilation of the Document or its derivatives with other separate and independent documents or works, in or on a volume of a storage or distribution medium, is called an "aggregate" if the copyright resulting from the compilation is not used to limit the legal rights of the compilation's users beyond what the individual works permit. When the Document is included in an aggregate, this License does not apply to the other works in the aggregate which are not themselves derivative works of the Document.

License

If the Cover Text requirement of section 3 is applicable to these copies of the Document, then if the Document is less than one half of the entire aggregate, the Document's Cover Texts may be placed on covers that bracket the Document within the aggregate, or the electronic equivalent of covers if the Document is in electronic form. Otherwise they must appear on printed covers that bracket the whole aggregate.

8. TRANSLATION

Translation is considered a kind of modification, so you may distribute translations of the Document under the terms of section 4. Replacing Invariant Sections with translations requires special permission from their copyright holders, but you may include translations of some or all Invariant Sections in addition to the original versions of these Invariant Sections. You may include a translation of this License, and all the license notices in the Document, and any Warranty Disclaimers, provided that you also include the original English version of this License and the original versions of those notices and disclaimers. In case of a disagreement between the translation and the original version of this License or a notice or disclaimer, the original version will prevail.

If a section in the Document is Entitled "Acknowledgements", "Dedications", or "History", the requirement (section 4) to Preserve its Title (section 1) will typically require changing the actual title.

9. TERMINATION

You may not copy, modify, sublicense, or distribute the Document except as expressly provided under this License. Any attempt otherwise to copy, modify, sublicense, or distribute it is void, and will automatically terminate your rights under this License.

However, if you cease all violation of this License, then your license from a particular copyright holder is reinstated (a) provisionally, unless and until the copyright holder explicitly and finally terminates your license, and (b) permanently, if the copyright holder fails to notify you of the violation by some reasonable means prior to 60 days after the cessation.

Moreover, your license from a particular copyright holder is reinstated permanently if the copyright holder notifies you of the violation by some reasonable means, this is the first time you have received notice of violation of this License (for any work) from that copyright holder, and you cure the violation prior to 30 days after your receipt of the notice.

Termination of your rights under this section does not terminate the licenses of parties who have received copies or rights from you under this License. If your rights have been terminated and not permanently reinstated, receipt of a copy of some or all of the same material does not give you any rights to use it.

10. FUTURE REVISIONS OF THIS LICENSE

The Free Software Foundation may publish new, revised versions of the GNU Free Documentation License from time to time. Such new versions will be similar in spirit to the present version, but may differ in detail to address new problems or concerns. See http://www.gnu.org/copyleft/.

Each version of the License is given a distinguishing version number. If the Document specifies that a particular numbered version of this License "or any later version" applies to it, you have the option of following the terms and conditions either of that specified version or of any later version that has been published (not as a draft) by the Free Software Foundation. If the Document does not specify a version number of this License, you may choose any version ever published (not as a draft) by the Free Software Foundation. If the Document specifies that a proxy can decide which future versions of this License can be used, that proxy's public statement of acceptance of a version permanently authorizes you to choose that version for the Document.

11. RELICENSING

"Massive Multiauthor Collaboration Site" (or "MMC Site") means any World Wide Web server that publishes copyrightable works and also provides prominent facilities for anybody to edit those works. A public wiki that anybody can edit is an example of such a server. A "Massive Multiauthor Collaboration" (or "MMC") contained in the site means any set of copyrightable works thus published on the MMC site.

"CC-BY-SA" means the Creative Commons Attribution-Share Alike 3.0 license published by Creative Commons Corporation, a not-for-profit corporation with a principal place of business in San Francisco, California, as well as future copyleft versions of that license published by that same organization.

"Incorporate" means to publish or republish a Document, in whole or in part, as part of another Document.

An MMC is "eligible for relicensing" if it is licensed under this License, and if all works that were first published under this License somewhere other than this MMC, and subsequently incorporated in whole or in part into the MMC, (1) had no cover texts or invariant sections, and (2) were thus incorporated prior to November 1, 2008.

The operator of an MMC Site may republish an MMC contained in the site under CC-BY-SA on the same site at any time before August 1, 2009, provided the MMC is eligible for relicensing.

How to use this License for your documents

To use this License in a document you have written, include a copy of the License in the document and put the following copyright and license notices just after the title page:

> Copyright (c) YEAR YOUR NAME.
> Permission is granted to copy, distribute and/or modify this document
> under the terms of the GNU Free Documentation License, Version 1.3
> or any later version published by the Free Software Foundation;
> with no Invariant Sections, no Front-Cover Texts, and no Back-Cover Texts.
> A copy of the license is included in the section entitled "GNU
> Free Documentation License".

If you have Invariant Sections, Front-Cover Texts and Back-Cover Texts, replace the "with...Texts." line with this:

> with the Invariant Sections being LIST THEIR TITLES, with the
> Front-Cover Texts being LIST, and with the Back-Cover Texts being LIST.

If you have Invariant Sections without Cover Texts, or some other combination of the three, merge those two alternatives to suit the situation.

If your document contains nontrivial examples of program code, we recommend releasing these examples in parallel under your choice of free software license, such as the GNU General Public License, to permit their use in free software.

GNU Free Documentation License Version 1.2, November 2002 Copyright (C) 2000,2001,2002 Free Software Foundation, Inc. 59 Temple Place, Suite 330, Boston, MA 02111-1307 USA Everyone is permitted to copy and distribute verbatim copies of this license document, but changing it is not allowed.

0. PREAMBLE
The purpose of this License is to make a manual, textbook, or other functional and useful document "free" in the sense of freedom: to assure everyone the effective freedom to copy and redistribute it, with or without modifying it, either commercially or noncommercially. Secondarily, this License preserves for the author and publisher a way to get credit for their work, while not being considered responsible for modifications made by others. This License is a kind of "copyleft", which means that derivative works of the document must themselves be free in the same sense. It complements the GNU General Public License, which is a copyleft license designed for free software. We have designed this License in order to use it for manuals for free software, because free software needs free documentation: a free program should come with manuals providing the same freedoms that the software does. But this License is not limited to software manuals; it can be used for any textual work, regardless of subject matter or whether it is published as a printed book. We recommend this License principally for works whose purpose is instruction or reference.

1. APPLICABILITY AND DEFINITIONS
This License applies to any manual or other work, in any medium, that contains a notice placed by the copyright holder saying it can be distributed under the terms of this License. Such a notice grants a world-wide, royalty-free license, unlimited in duration, to use that work under the conditions stated herein. The "Document", below, refers to any such manual or work. Any member of the public is a licensee, and is addressed as "you". You accept the license if you copy, modify or distribute the work in a way requiring permission under copyright law. A "Modified Version" of the Document means any work containing the Document or a portion of it, either copied verbatim, or with modifications and/or translated into another language. A "Secondary Section" is a named appendix or a front-matter section of the Document that deals exclusively with the relationship of the publishers or authors of the Document to the Document's overall subject (or to related matters) and contains nothing that could fall directly within that overall subject. (Thus, if the Document is in part a textbook of mathematics, a Secondary Section may not explain any mathematics.) The relationship could be a matter of historical connection with the subject or with related matters, or of legal, commercial, philosophical, ethical or political position regarding them. The "Invariant Sections" are certain Secondary Sections whose titles are designated, as being those of Invariant Sections, in the notice that says that the Document is released under this License. If a section does not fit the above definition of Secondary then it is not allowed to be designated as Invariant. The Document may contain zero Invariant Sections. If the Document does not identify any Invariant Sections then there are none. The "Cover Texts" are certain short passages of text that are listed, as Front-Cover Texts or Back-Cover Texts, in the notice that says that the Document is released under this License. A Front-Cover Text may be at most 5 words, and a Back-Cover Text may be at most 25 words. A "Transparent" copy of the Document means a machine-readable copy, represented in a format whose specification is available to the general public, that is suitable for revising the document straightforwardly with generic text editors or (for images composed of pixels) generic paint programs or (for drawings) some widely available drawing editor, and that is suitable for input to text formatters or for automatic translation to a variety of formats suitable for input to text formatters. A copy made in an otherwise Transparent file format whose markup, or absence of markup, has been arranged to thwart or discourage subsequent modification by readers is not Transparent. An image format is not Transparent if used for any substantial amount of text. A copy that is not "Transparent" is called "Opaque". Examples of suitable formats for Transparent copies include plain ASCII without markup, Texinfo input format, LaTeX input format, SGML or XML using a publicly available DTD, and standard-conforming simple HTML, PostScript or PDF designed for human modification. Examples of transparent image formats include PNG, XCF and JPG. Opaque formats include proprietary formats that can be read and edited only by proprietary word processors, SGML or XML for which the DTD and/or processing tools are not generally available, and the machine-generated HTML, PostScript or PDF produced by some word processors for output purposes only. The "Title Page" means, for a printed book, the title page itself, plus such following pages as are needed to hold, legibly, the material this License requires to appear in the title page. For works in formats which do not have any title page as such, "Title Page" means the text near the most prominent appearance of the work's title, preceding the beginning of the body of the text. A section "Entitled XYZ" means a named subunit of the Document whose title either is precisely XYZ or contains XYZ in parentheses following text that translates XYZ in another language. (Here XYZ stands for a specific section name mentioned below, such as "Acknowledgements", "Dedications", "Endorsements", or "History".) To "Preserve the Title" of such a section when you modify the Document means that it remains a section "Entitled XYZ" according to this definition. The Document may include Warranty Disclaimers next to the notice which states that this License applies to the Document. These Warranty Disclaimers are considered to be included by reference in this License, but only as regards disclaiming warranties: any other implication that these Warranty Disclaimers may have is void and has no effect on the meaning of this License.

2. VERBATIM COPYING
You may copy and distribute the Document in any medium, either commercially or noncommercially, provided that this License, the copyright notices, and the license notice saying this License applies to the Document are reproduced in all copies, and that you add no other conditions whatsoever to those of this License. You may not use technical measures to obstruct or control the reading or further copying of the copies you make or distribute. However, you may accept compensation in exchange for copies. If you distribute a large enough number of copies you must also follow the conditions in section 3. You may also lend copies, under the same conditions stated above, and you may publicly display copies.

3. COPYING IN QUANTITY
If you publish printed copies (or copies in media that commonly have printed covers) of the Document, numbering more than 100, and the Document's license notice requires Cover Texts, you must enclose the copies in covers that carry, clearly and legibly, all these Cover Texts: Front-Cover Texts on the front cover, and Back-Cover Texts on the back cover. Both covers must also clearly and legibly identify you as the publisher of these copies. The front cover must present the full title with all words of the title equally prominent and visible. You may add other material on the covers in addition. Copying with changes limited to the covers, as long as they preserve the title of the Document and satisfy these conditions, can be treated as verbatim copying in other respects. If the required texts for either cover are too voluminous to fit legibly, you should put the first ones listed (as many as fit reasonably) on the actual cover, and continue the rest onto adjacent pages. If you publish or distribute Opaque copies of the Document numbering more than 100, you must either include a machine-readable Transparent copy along with each Opaque copy, or state in or with each Opaque copy a computer-network location from which the general network-using public has access to download using public-standard network protocols a complete Transparent copy of the Document, free of added material. If you use the latter option, you must take reasonably prudent steps, when you begin distribution of Opaque copies in quantity, to ensure that this Transparent copy will remain thus accessible at the stated location until at least one year after the last time you distribute an Opaque copy (directly or through your agents or retailers) of that edition to the public. It is requested, but not required, that you contact the authors of the Document well before redistributing any large number of copies, to give them a chance to provide you with an updated version of the Document.

4. MODIFICATIONS
You may copy and distribute a Modified Version of the Document under the conditions of sections 2 and 3 above, provided that you release the Modified Version under precisely this License, with the Modified Version filling the role of the Document, thus licensing distribution and modification of the Modified Version to whoever possesses a copy of it. In addition, you must do these things in the Modified Version: A. Use in the Title Page (and on the covers, if any) a title distinct from that of the Document, and from those of previous versions (which should, if there were any, be listed in the History section of the Document). You may use the same title as a previous version if the original publisher of that version gives permission. B. List on the Title Page, as authors, one or more persons or entities responsible for authorship of the modifications in the Modified Version, together with at least five of the principal authors of the Document (all of its principal authors, if it has fewer than five), unless they release you from this requirement. C. State on the Title page the name of the publisher of the Modified Version, as the publisher. D. Preserve all the copyright notices of the Document. E. Add an appropriate copyright notice for your modifications adjacent to the other copyright notices. F. Include, immediately after the copyright notices, a license notice giving the public permission to use the Modified Version under the terms of this License, in the form shown in the Addendum below. G. Preserve in that license notice the full lists of Invariant Sections and required Cover Texts given in the Document's license notice. H. Include an unaltered copy of this License. I. Preserve the section Entitled "History", Preserve its Title, and add to it an item stating at least the title, year, new authors, and publisher of the Modified Version as given on the Title Page. If there is no section Entitled "History" in the Document, create one stating the title, year, authors, and publisher of the Document as given on its Title Page, then add an item describing the Modified Version as stated in the previous sentence. J. Preserve the network location, if any, given in the Document for public access to a Transparent copy of the Document, and likewise the network locations given in the Document for previous versions it was based on. These may be placed in the "History" section. You may omit a network location for a work that was published at least four years before the Document itself, or if the original publisher of the version it refers to gives permission. K. For any section Entitled "Acknowledgements" or "Dedications", Preserve the Title of the section, and preserve in the section all the substance and tone of each of the contributor acknowledgements and/or dedications given therein. L. Preserve all the Invariant Sections of the Document, unaltered in their text and in their titles. Section numbers or the equivalent are not considered part of the section titles. M. Delete any section Entitled "Endorsements". Such a section may not be included in the Modified Version. N. Do not retitle any existing section to be Entitled "Endorsements" or to conflict in title with any Invariant Section. O. Preserve any Warranty Disclaimers. If the Modified Version includes new front-matter sections or appendices that qualify as Secondary Sections and contain no material copied from the Document, you may at your option designate some or all of these sections as invariant. To do this, add their titles to the list of Invariant Sections in the Modified Version's license notice. These titles must be distinct from any other section titles. You may add a section Entitled "Endorsements", provided it contains nothing but endorsements of your Modified Version by various parties--for example, statements of peer review or that the text has been approved by an organization as the authoritative definition of a standard. You may add a passage of up to five words as a Front-Cover Text, and a passage of up to 25 words as a Back-Cover Text, to the end of the list of Cover Texts in the Modified Version. Only one passage of Front-Cover Text and one of Back-Cover Text may be added by (or through arrangements made by) any one entity. If the Document already includes a cover text for the same cover, previously added by you or by arrangement made by the same entity you are acting on behalf of, you may not add another; but you may replace the old one, on explicit permission from the previous publisher that added the old one. The author(s) and publisher(s) of the Document do not by this License give permission to use their names for publicity for or to assert or imply endorsement of any Modified Version.

5. COMBINING DOCUMENTS
You may combine the Document with other documents released under this License, under the terms defined in section 4 above for modified versions, provided that you include in the combination all of the Invariant Sections of all of the original documents, unmodified, and list them all as Invariant Sections of your combined work in its license notice, and that you preserve all their Warranty Disclaimers. The combined work need only contain one copy of this License, and multiple identical Invariant Sections may be replaced with a single copy. If there are multiple Invariant Sections with the same name but different contents, make the title of each such section unique by adding at the end of it, in parentheses, the name of the original author or publisher of that section if known, or else a unique number. Make the same adjustment to the section titles in the list of Invariant Sections in the license notice of the combined work. In the combination, you must combine any sections Entitled "History" in the various original documents, forming one section Entitled "History"; likewise combine any sections Entitled "Acknowledgements", and any sections Entitled "Dedications". You must delete all sections Entitled "Endorsements".

6. COLLECTIONS OF DOCUMENTS
You may make a collection consisting of the Document and other documents released under this License, and replace the individual copies of this License in the various documents with a single copy that is included in the collection, provided that you follow the rules of this License for verbatim copying of each of the documents in all other respects. You may extract a single document from such a collection, and distribute it individually under this License, provided you insert a copy of this License into the extracted document, and follow this License in all other respects regarding verbatim copying of that document.

7. AGGREGATION WITH INDEPENDENT WORKS
A compilation of the Document or its derivatives with other separate and independent documents or works, in or on a volume of a storage or distribution medium, is called an "aggregate" if the copyright resulting from the compilation is not used to limit the legal rights of the compilation's users beyond what the individual works permit. When the Document is included in an aggregate, this License does not apply to the other works in the aggregate which are not themselves derivative works of the Document. If the Cover Text requirement of section 3 is applicable to these copies of the Document, then if the Document is less than one half of the entire aggregate, the Document's Cover Texts may be placed on covers that bracket the Document within the aggregate, or the electronic equivalent of covers if the Document is in electronic form. Otherwise they must appear on printed covers that bracket the whole aggregate.

8. TRANSLATION
Translation is considered a kind of modification, so you may distribute translations of the Document under the terms of section 4. Replacing Invariant Sections with translations requires special permission from their copyright holders, but you may include translations of some or all Invariant Sections in addition to the original versions of these Invariant Sections. You may include a translation of this License, and all the license notices in the Document, and any Warranty Disclaimers, provided that you also include the original English version of this License and the original versions of those notices and disclaimers. In case of a disagreement between the translation and the original version of this License or a notice or disclaimer, the original version will prevail. If a section in the Document is Entitled "Acknowledgements", "Dedications", or "History", the requirement (section 4) to Preserve its Title (section 1) will typically require changing the actual title.

9. TERMINATION
You may not copy, modify, sublicense, or distribute the Document except as expressly provided for under this License. Any other attempt to copy, modify, sublicense or distribute the Document is void, and will automatically terminate your rights under this License. However, parties who have received copies, or rights, from you under this License will not have their licenses terminated so long as such parties remain in full compliance.

10. FUTURE REVISIONS OF THIS LICENSE
The Free Software Foundation may publish new, revised versions of the GNU Free Documentation License from time to time. Such new versions will be similar in spirit to the present version, but may differ in detail to address new problems or concerns. See http://www.gnu.org/copyleft/. Each version of the License is given a distinguishing version number. If the Document specifies that a particular numbered version of this License "or any later version" applies to it, you have the option of following the terms and conditions either of that specified version or of any later version that has been published (not as a draft) by the Free Software Foundation. If the Document does not specify a version number of this License, you may choose any version ever published (not as a draft) by the Free Software Foundation. ADDENDUM: How to use this License for your documents To use this License in a document you have written, include a copy of the License in the document and put the following copyright and license notices just after the title page: Copyright (c) YEAR YOUR NAME. Permission is granted to copy, distribute and/or modify this document under the terms of the GNU Free Documentation License, Version 1.2 or any later version published by the Free Software Foundation; with no Invariant Sections, no Front-Cover Texts, and no Back-Cover Texts. A copy of the license is included in the section entitled "GNU Free Documentation License". If you have Invariant Sections, Front-Cover Texts and Back-Cover Texts, replace the "with..Texts." line with this: with the Invariant Sections being LIST THEIR TITLES, with the Front-Cover Texts being LIST, and with the Back-Cover Texts being LIST. If you have Invariant Sections without Cover Texts, or some other combination of the three, merge those two alternatives to suit the situation. If your document contains nontrivial examples of program code, we recommend releasing these examples in parallel under your choice of free software license, such as the GNU General Public License, to permit their use in free software.

CPSIA information can be obtained at www.ICGtesting.com
Printed in the USA
BVOW042323230513

321524BV00004BA/269/P